# No Doubts Here!

A Collection of Essays, Poems and Letters
## MERICE COLE, M.S.

Becoming 50Something Publications

Email: **50somethinglifestyle@gmail.com**

Website: 50somethinglifestyle.com

ISBN: 979-8-218-08940-5

## Junction 1

My joy is to inspire my readers to move from promise to purpose in your land with intentions, integrity, love, honesty and liberty for your liberation.

## Junction 2

It is my desire to lead you to muse through revaluations of rhymes, rhythmic blues, and transformational verses.

## Junction 3

I promise to send your senses into realistic thresholds of well worth treasures and blessings.

## Junction 4

My hope is my work will cause you to think, take action, and find a space to be an influencer with solutions.

## Merice Cole

# DEDICATION

I truly believe that without the help of all my supporting cast members, this work would not be possible. First, I want to sincerely thank my daughter Alex, a dedicated student to your dreams. You are a mom to Harper, a partner to Martin, and a super encourager to me. You are a remarkable and sophisticated woman to everyone around you.

To my mom, your God-fearing bravery and tenacity are strengths your children draw from. You are an awesome example to us. To my dad, God bless his heart, who has gone on to be with the Lord. He was a great father to his seven children.

I also dedicate this book to my sister Jennifer, an awesome mom and a woman who lifts my spirit countless times. To Gillian my strong-willed sister who has a good heart and is a very supportive mom; and my sister-in-law Rhina, the woman who cares for all of us and makes sure I'm taking care of myself. She lives unselfishly without a doubt.

To my dear Robyn, my secret superpower, I thank you for helping me to stand up. To my external family: Myrandia, Melinda, Gentry, Brooke, and Brandon. Myrandia you are my sister from another mother, a staple, a light in my path. To my family on the other side, and my Mama Hill whom I thank God for her strength and grace. I love you all, my heart swells with gratitude.

Also, to my brothers Everton, Carlton, Winston, and Ruel, the quiet storm in my life and a giant in my world. You guys make our family an amazing place to be. To my nephew RJ and Ambar. RJ, you have read just about everything I have written. You were my light when I sometimes felt darkness in my writings.

To my core, close friends and school family. Thank you for your encouragement. You uplift my spirit on so many occasions.

Lastly, without a doubt, to the power of the Living God without whose continued love, favor, blessings, and direction this work would not have been possible.

Special thank you to Mr. Maurice Howard for the fantastic book cover art. He is an awesome artist and deserves to be acknowledged.

# CONTENTS

INTRODUCTION........................................................................ 1
FAITH ..................................................................................... 4
Birds of broken wings ............................................................ 6
Deborah and Barak in Judges 4 and 5 ................................... 8
God's divine Intervention....................................................... 10
He is so faithful, He can't fail ............................................... 18
Who are you affiliated with? ..................................................21
Sometimes we weep because we seek.................................... 23
Unlock your mental capacity.................................................. 24
What is your cause? Acts 19 ...................................................25
Your destination is a victory ..................................................27
SISTERHOOD ........................................................................ 30
An unwelcomed intrusion to my womanhood ....................... 30
His obsession became a pre-occupation................................. 32
I ain't store-bought! ............................................................... 33
Ladies, "here I am"................................................................ 34
Own you first........................................................................ 36
Sisters ................................................................................... 39
We strut that beat! ................................................................. 41
The flower that blossomed and bloomed .............................. 43
The loneliness of a coveted wife ........................................... 47
This world is your canvas....................................................... 49
I know a Shero....................................................................... 51
GRATITUDE .......................................................................... 54
Beach day .............................................................................. 54
Love ambushed and trapped her almost to death .................. 56
Love's confidence ................................................................. 59
Not today .............................................................................. 60
One's attitude is everything.................................................... 62
A letter to mom ..................................................................... 64
Don't get her wrong .............................................................. 66
Obligated for life .................................................................. 67
The bitter sweetness of sisterhood......................................... 70
CULTURE .............................................................................. 72
Buried freedom will translate into life's disruption .............. 72

We the people have rights "without black codes" ........................76
The entertainer's footprints ............................................77
The reckoning with my reality (behind the orange curtain) ..........79
The wind.................................................................81
White "people's" premise of privilege .................................83
As we are ...............................................................85
L A X, why am I in trauma?..............................................88
Black love...............................................................89
HUMANITY ...............................................................92
Assessing one's value...................................................92
Caught by a mouse ......................................................94
Every life is a descendant from an earlier life .......................95
The deadliest kind of ambition.........................................96
Sojourners in a passage called life....................................98
I'm intrigued..........................................................101
It looks like competition, but the reflection is fear.................103
The weed that serenaded the rose ......................................105
Discovering values ....................................................107
Water is a living source ..............................................108
About the Author.......................................................110

# INTRODUCTION

Hello to all my spectacular, gifted, and loved friends! Our lives are a beautiful tapestry of experiences. Everyone has a unique quest to experience, yet many paths will cross. *No Doubts Here* speaks to no debilitating, opposing, unreliable, or beastly thinking that will discourage us from dependency to independence. God provides resources and breakthroughs to help us succeed and prosper. God is always working on our behalf, no matter the time, place, space, or circumstances we face. This project became a book before I started writing its contents in conversations. My appreciation and gratitude belong to my international family, internal and externa, and Alex, my highly exceptionally, incredibly gifted daughter.

My inner circle of friends serves as eyewitnesses to the monumental role COVID-19 played in our lives over the last two years. Please allow this body of work to bless and know that knowledge, wisdom, and understanding is a gift from God, not from humankind. In the book of life, John 1:4 states: "In him was life, and the life was the light of men."

This nation we consider home, the United States of America, is a perplexing monument of love, hate, and betrayal to lives lived and lost. I am grateful for this opportunity to introduce a different personification of life's activities. And as we continue the journey to challenge ourselves to think beyond individualism and self-imposed ideology, let's resist the expectations of competitive spirits of cultural impossibilities, and instead remedy the history of injustice through a homogeneous reality.

It is essential to recognize and remember the trials that make us remarkable achievers. Let's commit to being greater and know that excellence is the only stability for a robust future. Let's be open to opportunities to express and explore how communities communicate with tools in dramatic statements of life's conflicts and progress in poetic references. I aim to build a momentum of confidence in your interpretation as you read. Welcome to *No Doubt Here*. Some may attempt to limit your mind by limiting your freedom. We must remain disciplined to continue the quest to be one nation under God!

The following piece of work registers reflection of the brutal truth Americans faced about the lack of respect and disregard to courage shared in a governing body authorized to empower and serve its people first. But, without a doubt, temperaments became the overwhelming justification for injustice to those without fortunes. Welcome to the beginning of a shared frontier of untampered philosophy of my mind. The following writing shows the difference between our diversity and our actual experiences. They emerge from one spirit—the spirit of a higher power. There are diversities within our activities, but the same God works all in all. My words are a gift that bears witness to assist others, not just myself. Words of wisdom- always informational with shared knowledge comes with a solution. Revaluation gifts is the ability to work through the spirit of God to generate a positive impact in the world around us. My goal is to win friends and influence people to experience the love of God without reservation, leaving my readers wholly satisfied. The position of boring is a conflict of interest to my readers. I want to build a momentum of confidence to impact, touch, and energize with trust to pull in the echoes of how you connect as you read because love conquers all! Please think of "Your" someone to love as you read each piece.

Reference page
https://stjohnsbaptistchurch.org/sermons/the-trustworthy-hand-of-god-october-10-2021/
https://stjohnsbaptistchurch.org/sermons/the-trustworthy-hand-of-god-october-10-2021/
https://www.un.org/sg/en/content/sg/statement/2017-10-11/secretary-generals-remarks-fifth-committee-general-assembly-proposed

FAITH

# FAITH

*I am not at the mercy of any human being; I am at the mercy of the hands of God the Father.*

You were created in God's image, not in your imagination as figments of someone else' imagination to be trolled upon. Under whose watch was it determined that your small chops are our distinguishing filter of hope? The Bible says, "For God so loved the world that He gave his only begotten son, that whosoever believeth in Him shall not perish but have everlasting life." This was not a man-made decision.

So, in your limited ability, you have chosen to interpret our fate. When did you become our god, inflicting righteous indignations in varying measures of insecurities at your discretion? Did we miss something as a people?

Who cast the burden of property ownership as to our suitability to disqualify, leaving us as the sole authority figures to deny others the right to prosper without dignity? Your supposition of prosecution is mystifying to the heart of my people, saith the Lord. Your presumption of ownership of my creation is an absolute abomination to the gift of life I gave. I have caused you to suffer at the hands of your own demise. In Philippians 4:5-6, God gives us clear directions. "Let your gentleness be known to all men. Be anxious for nothing, but in everything by prayer and supplication, with thanksgiving, let your request be made known to God."

His peace and His understanding will surpass all human understanding.

Unfortunately, we have not learned to release and rely on the biblical application of our leaders in this time of a perilous, infectious virus. As long as we guard our hearts and minds through Christ Jesus, do nothing from a human understanding. Ephesians 6:6-8 says, "Not with eye service, as men-pleasers, but as the

4

servants of Christ, doing the will of God from the heart. With good will doing service, as to the Lord, and not to men: knowing that whatever good thing any man doeth, the same shall he receive of the Lord, whether he be bond, or free."

We have become so self-righteous, giving ourselves the right to do as we please. Not recognizing that God had to stop us dead in our tracks. Yet so many of us have continued to take on the nobility of I am bigger than our creator and struggle to make the connection of His greatness.

America continues to operate under the espoused assumption that my riches are my destiny. And has once again removed itself from God's daily mercies. His arms are outstretched. Those who are willing will be covered. When will we recoil from our distrustful nature and bow down to His grace? Take a knee to the almighty that is our confident conqueror, our help in times of distress, and recognize His awesomeness in the way he continues to be of service to our brokenness.

# Birds of broken wings

A bird cannot take flight when one of its wings is impaired. Flying is the natural precept in the foundation of a baby bird's release into its revelation. Birds of broken wings are not equipped to flourish under this circumstance. The power of equilibrium is vital to balancing a bird's symmetry. God designed birds to fly in a V formation, which is relevant to the success of their favored destination. Researchers have found that birds share the tiring lead position in their V formations. It takes a flock to fly. A recent paper by Voelkl and colleagues revealed the northern bald ibis flies in a V to get a little extra lift from the birds in front of them. (February 3, 2015.)

As children of the Living God, we must be present in His abundant grace to move to our destination. It is contingent upon our belief that we acknowledge His time, space, and grace. His promises will usher us into our rightful positions before flying into our destiny. So, just wait.

The clipping of our wings is only a distraction. Bound or broken, we will find a way to navigate the past, present, and future of our purpose, desires, and dreams. God wants to give us the information through His word, so don't let it become a weight. We must be open and available to receive love. It is a measure of patience in our favor, and it comes with a distinct flavor. Chastisements, although challenging, will be empowering. So don't resent allowing vulnerability to open and grow our faith. It is vitally essential in times of testing, so digest and savor.

The head must have a tremendous amount of gratitude to the rest of the flock for the outcome to be successful. It is a shared duty. That is why God has given us the responsibility and opportunity of redemption to fly in His flock to see our beauty. We are sometimes birds with broken wings and hearts. We aspire to fly in a V formation to increase our strength through His promises, and this is where we start. The one in front carries the bulk of the weight, but it is also important for the rest of the group to see it as a privilege to keep the formation unified. Without unity, the destination is impossible to chart.

We have a fighting chance in God's Grace if we first forgive any harm inflicted and embrace our ability to be magnificent and smart. I am so intensely blessed to be a warrior, a survivor of many intentional and unintentional behaviors by others. I am overwhelmingly grateful for disruptive remarks that had the potential to mislead and destroy my roadmap. There were times when I had to restart. At times, I became distracted by my thoughts.

This piece of meaningful information was shared with me in my earlier years as a teacher's assistant, working with students who suffered neglect at the hands of the adults who should have had their best interests at heart. However, these students were instead discarded. My mentor was the principal of the school where I worked. Her wisdom and experiences gave us insight into the population we dealt with. Her position, coupled with love and a wealth of valuable information was remarkably beneficial as she took the time to mentor us.

This information was intended to aid our capacity; if we wanted to be influential and committed to applying the appropriate teaching tools to our students. She stated, "every child has been equipped with an instinct to survive, but once that internal baby gets distorted and has redistributed to meaningless wastelands, it's impossible to regenerate."

We will encounter dysfunction at its worst. So, look for the baby who has been destroyed and redirect to integrate. Work intending to nurture and protect that which can be rebuilt and build an adequate foundation to thrive positively and relate. Birds with broken wings cannot and will not get off the ground. Unless there is hope in you to enhance and improve with impact. Gently cradle the future of the lives you touch with heavenly hearts and hands like birds with broken wings. These are the children we serve because their lives are profoundly valuable if we want them to stand intact.

# Deborah and Barak in Judges 4 and 5

A woman of power and purpose, she had no fear of failure. Listen to why you are called for such a time as this, as Mordecai reminded Esther in her purpose to protect her people from destruction.

Never underestimate the power of the living God. He uses the most unlikely source to achieve his goal.

His goal is to bless and replenish our strength with soundness.

Deborah was a woman of action and substance. She was a ruler, leader, judge, wife, and warrior. She understood her position and recognized that nothing is accomplished through self-reliance. Barak was the essence of things hoped for not going headstrong into a battle without protection; Deborah was aware of God's plan.

A plan for a future and hope. She did not declare this undertaking as a personal vendetta. Deborah conceived this conquest through her faithfulness to bring about peace to a nation in turmoil and unrest.

Barak was a significant contributor to that victory; this was a test. Although it appears that he was intimidated by force on the other side of the war, he knew that Deborah's purpose and position were vital to the win; he had to go the distance.

His role as a prominent soldier was necessary for what God intended. Sometimes we are so invested in our internal voices and outside noises that we lose sight of the intervention we need to succeed.

Our attitudes about selfishness will always distract, distort, and destroy the intended purpose. In addition, we sell ourselves short sometimes to failure of sorts.

I'm sure that as a man, Barak's interpretation of Deborah's suggestion was as lofty as any man's. Still, he avidly trusted her vision and integrity as he carried out the plan.

Deborah realized Barak was her confidante, an ally, and a friend, but more importantly, he was a prepared military man with wisdom and courage. In contrast, this was not his first battle of the bands. God had prepared him in prior experiences to fight. As long as she was by his side, he would abide and not discourage.

The reality of teamwork takes effort to achieve the desired effect, but only through a consensus agreement from all parties involved. It cannot be reckless. Whether it is in a love interest or platonic relationship, it's a commitment in which you are determined to stand. Any endeavors we undertake, including relationships, require a conscientious effort, not a grandstand.

Nothing is ever effortless. It takes perseverance and hard work to achieve your goals, dreams, or ambitions through confidence and faith in our God of old. Deborah lacked nothing in her climb to represent her people and God's call to His righteousness; she did not fall.

Love, live, and thrive in your purpose to empower. For God will impart His superpower.

# God's divine intervention

As I chronicle my diagnosis with the coronavirus, I give thanks to my Heavenly Father. The God above seeks to assure us of His unconditional love and healing over our lives. He offered a blessing to me on this day, and it is the gift of life. My heart is full of gratitude and thanksgiving. I have realized how much God loves me. In His omnipotent survey of who I am, He claims me; I belong to Him. His words were to me, "I give you life for such a time as this."

On December 29, 2020, I began feeling uneasy, with a mild clammy sensation. Not a fever, but with a scratchy throat. That same Tuesday evening, a church member sent me a video of a pastor from Africa. Something in my spirit moved me to listen to the word of God and it infiltrated the core of my being. It touched my heart with sincerity.

The next day, December 31, 2020, I took the COVID test and received the result from the surgery center as positive. God said to me, "I have killed the root of that which touches you." I immediately retreated to isolation. I went to my room and did my fourteen-day stay. I stayed as far away from my daughter as possible. I also called my doctor to deliver the essential and crushing news.

I felt a little down but continued to rebound comfortably in my faith. I had a slight temperature of 99.4. I took a couple of doses of Tylenol and felt better throughout the day. As the evening drew near, I started experiencing a slight headache, and I used the comfrey root, which alleviated the headache. On New Year's Day, I was awakened to begin writing my journey with this uninvited, unwelcome experience. Here is my journey:

January 1, 2021: Today I have a slight headache, coughing slightly, with some mucus in my throat. I got up and went into the kitchen to make the broth, as I refer to it as my COVID tea. My mom gave me the recipe. It includes ginger, lemon peel, orange peel, basil leaves, turmeric, garlic, and comfrey root.

I am excited to be alive today. My gratitude is unwavering in so many ways, for I am grateful for blessings. After all, it is New Year's Day. I do not have a temperature today, and I thank God. As my day ensues, conversations I have with people I communicate with frequently, leave me a little intimidated. I quietly embark on some conversations with strength. Others I engage with uncommon anxiety. After one particular conversation, I felt like I needed reassurance because I was unusually nervous that I had to call my brother to examine my breathing for stress. Glory be to God that I am in good standing per his findings. I went to bed and slept quite well.

January 2, 2021: Today I am still observing, absorbing, and processing this strange, disturbing situation. With a tremendous amount of gratitude, I shower God with praise unselfishly. I have been shut away for days, although realistically, it has been a relatively short number of hours. The positive side of this is I am doing exceptionally well. I experienced some coughing and drainage in the back of my throat throughout the day, but nothing alarming to report. It has been my task to bring up as much phlegm as possible to rid myself of this cloud.

January 3, 2021: Today is Sunday, a day of thanksgiving and worship. With gratitude, I humble myself before the throne of God's grace. I woke up feeling very refreshed today. I do have some chest/throat phlegm happening this morning. It makes me recognize God holds all of our lives in His marvelous hands. I appreciate that there are patterns in how the body releases unwanted debris. Early in the morning, it sheds anything that may hamper your day, a new beginning by throwing off things that can impact your progress. Sometimes we are so busy that we don't notice how God works in our favor, discarding the things that stop or prevent us from getting the best of Him. I read Deuteronomy 12 and 13. Idols are not for the children of God. They serve no bearing purpose in our lives. They prevent us from reaching our true potential, and they are interceptors that cause us to be unstable.

I watched the video from my church today. It provides a tremendous amount of strength and relationship building, just knowing that God is in control of everything on this earth. .My breathing was intense, my lungs were clear, and I took a walk. Walks are my favorite things to do, and today is the first one I have had in several days. It feels great!! Walks are invigorating. I wanted to take a long one. Instead, I took a short 10-minute one.

January 4, 2021: My God asks the question. "Whose report will you believe, an invalid report?" His report is the only report I need. For me, God sits on the throne of all things possible. Alex's auntie sent me some Father John's cough medicine today. I greatly appreciate her for that. This is a day to trust in God's mercy and Grace. I take a second COVID test with the result available in 48 hours.

I believe my faith is in God's hands. He will do what He says He will do. I feel a small amount of uneasiness before leaving to take the test, but that is my human nature, fear of being told that the test will be the same as before. I will not be afraid, for God knows what is best. I am alive today, giving honor and gratitude to God for seeing me through another day. My daughter has been a trooper throughout this experience. Alex has been taking care of me daily, with no complaints. I am genuinely grateful for her. Thank you, Lord Jesus, for my child. I ask that you continue to cover her daily, strengthen her fortitude, and give her rest in you, oh Lord! My loving sister-in-law, my brother's wife, made the best soup ever today. I am so thankful that I have not lost my sense of smell or taste. God has been so faithful to me that His mercy always endures.

January 5, 2021: I woke up with a song in my heart by Tauren Wells, "Do what you are famous for." He continues to strengthen me daily, even when my unbelief wants to control my faith. I will not give in or let go of God's promises. He covers me and covers me. Today I will push through, no matter the situation. Watching the video from the pastor in Africa gives me insight into God's favor. I am thankful and blessed that God knows what we need. A song during the prayer says, "If God can't do it, If God can't fix it, if God can't solve it, it does not exist! For I know my redeemer lives."

I experienced a tremendous amount of anxiety today. Prayers are the most potent source of comfort to me. I read the book of James today. It was about how our faith works in times of trial. James 2:1 says: "Do not hold the faith of our Lord Jesus with partial thinking." My faith is the only action I need to put in place today. I am coughing, but I am feeling powerful in my breathing.

January 6, 2021: I am a little apprehensive about the test results in a day or so. No matter the outcome, God sits on the throne. I go for a walk in my driveway and backyard today, feeling pretty good. Alex also helps me put the oil mixture of onions under the bottom of my feet to help pull out toxins from my chest. Alex also takes her third COVID test today as well. I pray that too will be negative. Alex received her test results on Wednesday, and yes, glory to God up above it was negative.

January 6th, a day of gratitude, is my call of focus today. I listened to the message from the pastor and his co-pastor, just acknowledging that Father God is all I need to get through this day. I dedicate my prayer time to honor Him.

January 7, 2021: Today, I receive the second test result, and yes, it is positive. Never let your heart be troubled, for joy comes in the morning. I worship, pray, and spend time together with God which is my favorite pastimes these days. I watch tv, but my focus was on trusting in God for His favor over my life.

January 8, 2021: I woke up today with a terrible cough, so I reached out to my doctor. Dr. Lewis returned my call and expressed his sorrow regarding my condition. He called in a prescription for cough medicine for me today. Alex went to Target to pick it up for me. I love my daughter so very much; she is the best child any mother could have asked for. Lord Jesus, please continue to provide and protect her in her daily walk. Thank you, Oh Heavenly Father, for favor over her life.

January 9, 2021: Today, I listened to the pastor and his praise and worship team. They are such a marvelous inspiration for my daily prayer life. My gratitude goes beyond any questions I may ponder about whether God is real, God is alive, and I sit at His throne because I know my redeemer is alive and well. He shows up every day in my life. "What God cannot do does not exist."

It's Saturday. In retrospect, I'm feeling relatively enlightened today. I woke up somewhat domesticated; I stripped my room from top to bottom. I washed my linens, cleaned the floor in my room, and felt very gratified because I feel like I am finally moving ahead of the intruder bug. I took a short walk to open my lungs and strengthen my airways. I listened to a pastor from Africa today, "What God cannot do; does not exist." Today was a fantastic day.

January 10, 2021:Today is Sunday known as the hump day of this journey, and it starts as a pretty edgy morning. My cough is quite persistent today. I become anxiety-ridden by the middle of the day. Although it should be a day of jubilation! Sometimes we forget to fight for what we believe is our right to prosper. We allow shallow intrusions to filter into our ability to see beyond our right to thrive. When a wall like this virus presents itself, my belief and determination are the best weapons in rebellion that arises and tries to turn my power of protection into fear. Believe and trust that God is more significant than any problem you may face. I needed to hear that from my brother today, who reminds me that this too shall pass. I saw a number that left me somewhere between desolate and disparaging. I take my faith and send it sailing on the boat of rushed judgment in a moment of disfigured functionality.

I am grateful to my mother for having seven children. I get to have one that lives next door and loves his sister. My gratitude to my sister by marriage is something I truly appreciate as part of my journey, as she is lovely, loving and kindhearted, caring, and attentive to a fault. My daughter is a special kind of fantastic woman throughout this experience with me.

January 11, 2021: Today is a much better day. It is Monday and I stepped out the doors of my house to observe the most magnificent view of five beautiful birds canvassing the blue ranges of the sky. They circled the heavens as nothing I've ever observed before. The birds paraded in various formations, weaving in and out of orbit. They made circles, V formations, straight lines, and zigzagged across the sky. It was the most fantastic, fabulous engagement of birds in flight I have ever witnessed. I was awe-struck by their exceptional display and expression of my life in flight. They appeared to be eagles giving their respectful profound appreciation. I was delighted by this heavenly, once-in-a-lifetime performance.

The excitement made me think of God's marvelous works and I wonder how He fashioned this entire earth with His own hands. I am profoundly blessed to be wonderfully and magnificently made by God. I am grateful to be alive today. I returned home filled with God's majestic awesomeness. I watched a bit of TV for a while and considered everything possible. My breathing is in a much more improved, powerful place today. My cough is less threatening to my wellness; it appears to be weaning. I am hopeful for tomorrow. Tonight, I will continue to make use of the air moisturizer in my room. It helps to keep my breathing strong. I will sleep well tonight.

January 12, 2021: I am thankful for this day; day number twelve of this viral intruder in my life's journey. I am so blessed that I am excited and not experiencing any anxiety issues today. I went for a walk to expand my lungs and lift my spirit. I read my Bible and read a few chapters of "An Attitude of Gratitude" from Pastor Davy Clays-Tahoe, a friend of Pastor Koffe. I shared with my nephew RJ some of my journaling related to my journey in COVID-19 and I have been sequestered/isolated for the past twelve days, and it sometimes feels like I've been locked away for a lifetime. There are no interactions with people outside of my immediate family members, and these interactions are conducted from at least six-to-ten feet or more apart. My daughter Alex received her first dose of the COVID-19 vaccine today. I must be honest. The care given by family and friends has profoundly impacted my recovery.

January 13, 2021: I have leveled plenty of benefits during these thirteen days, along with a unique blend of care allowing me to heal. That kind of love has presented tremendous support through this process, and I am so grateful. Today is not a particularly industrious day. I spent the morning in prayer listening to Joel Osteen, reading the Bible, and being thankful that today is the thirteenth day of working through my journey with this potentially dangerous virus. I went for a walk that took me half of my usual hour time frame. Today is the first time in two weeks that I have been able to take such a more vigorous, eventful, purposeful, and steady walk. I walked for over thirty minutes today. It was refreshing and a beautiful, welcome feeling.

I received a text from Mama Hill that a very close friend of hers passed away earlier today. My heart goes out to both mama and Francine's family. I am grateful to God for everyone and every moment that He gives through His mercy and unrelenting grace. "What God cannot do; does not exist."

January 14, 2021: It is my passage day with coronavirus. It is a solemn day, a day of rest, a day of peace, and a day of praise. I am giving honor to God that he has carried me through the trenches with this dangerous disease. Dealing with this virus gives me assurance that God stands with us no matter what. I walked around the school down the street from my house, took a deep breath, and was so grateful. I am thankful to God for his mercy every day that this virus did not attack my lungs; it attacked me psychologically, but God walked me through this fire, and brought me back to the other side of the fireplace. That is what coronavirus felt like to me.

Understand that you're in a fireplace, and if God is not with you, it may be a dangerous place to be. So, I can't go it alone, without Grace and His mercy. Tomorrow I will take my test; the outcome will be according to what God brings. Amen!

January 15, 2021: I took the retest for the COVID virus! Lord, you carried me out of this fire, and now I'm a survivor of COVID-19, a new woman. Praise God! I am COVID-free!! The result is negative. I feel like I can breathe again; thank you, Jesus. And there is no going out to public places without a mask. Freedom feels amazing!

I received my first dose of the vaccine on February 27, 2021, and I look forward to getting the second dose on March 27, 2021. I chose the Moderna vaccine. While waiting in line, I was touched by the unimaginable amount of gifts God offers us daily. During this time, a song came to me, realizing that, as humans, it's a challenge to not dislike life feverishly. I was determined to unlock my pent-up emotions that attempted to overthrow me. God's divine intervention can happen at any moment in your life; be open to all of His possibilities.

I had not felt the touch of God in a long time. His work was being done on my behalf without my knowledge. He shows up in the most unprecedented, unpredictable situations or times when we don't expect Him. Thank you, my heavenly father. I offer my prayers beyond my ability to express them, as I am grateful for your deliverance. You become vulnerable to this disease, but during my episode with the virus, it was a challenge to focus. God can see things that threaten us long before we can see or ever phantom their reality. Lord, you bless us unconditionally, and all you ask of us is to acknowledge your love for us and respond in obedience. We will, in turn, live prosperously because in you is the only sovereign place.

This could have been a very different experience without your love for me; your intervention was critical to my recovery.

# He is so faithful, He can't fail

The joy that comes from knowing that God is standing behind, in front of, beside, and next to us is breathtaking. He is the best friend you or I will ever have. Just as breathing brings us closer to the presence of God, our prayers touch the heart of God. Our prayers are direct conversations and connections with Him. Though we may encounter many trials and tribulations, Christ is our center, our unmovable rock. We have no idea how He delivers, as He greets and moves our lives, even when we experience rugged terrains. We struggle through our best estimation and work to adjust our day each morning. He welcomes us with His incredible gift of life every day, measured only by the strength of our faith or mistakes. Let God wash over your life with His tenderness. God's favor is the salvation He offers you unconditionally. You want God to laugh; tell him your best-laid plans, and He will show you how underdeveloped and inadequate you are.

It was such an honor to watch a group of people from varied backgrounds on Monday during the Martin Luther King celebration day. It is a day of service for men, women, boys, and girls in this country to provide others with the purpose of passion.

I was not too surprised to find a pastor from the south with such a lofty vision. The idea was a fantastic, progressive way of thinking. He dared to envision a choir that would bring healing through gospel music. He declared his belief and worked with his nephew, Pharrell Williams, a superstar and highly recognized musical star in his own rights. I was impressed because the little I knew about Pharrell was that he was not from a gospel background. However, his uncle, Pastor Williams, envisioned creating a cross-cultural mass choir. He partnered with Pharrell and a tenacious choirmaster, Patrick Riddick; a well-known voice coach in the Virginia area, Peggy Britt; and a bright musical director, Larry George. This team of visionaries embraced and embarked on a critical mission to deliver joy to planet earth. As people, we desire to be re-energized from time to time.

He then put out a call for anyone interested in attending the audition. And the response was phenomenal. Singers with a desire to praise God introduced themselves by sharing their histories, stories, and their testimonies, which featured melodies from various regions of the East Coast to the back roads of Virginia. The "Voices of Fire" is a divinely appropriate name for such a magnificent group of people. As they shared their stories, they saw healing take shape in their own lives.

They persevered through tremendous challenges during rehearsals with bravado personalities. And, at the moment of truth, the day the choir debuted, the ensemble lit the stage, mesmerizing and defending their rightful place. Their voices reached an exploding crescendo, igniting tones and rhythmic scales. Each distinctive voice moved the audience as they marveled in worship.

The singers carried the most exquisitely delicate sounds in various renditions of gospel music in complete harmony. It was an exaltation of the highest magnitude, refreshing to the spirit. It was a beautiful experience. They were exciting, stimulating, moving, and motivating, excelling in their presentation. The faces of the attendees showed triumphant joy as the choir delivered songs from faraway places, including the high hills of Virginia, to the low plains of Georgia. Their voices transformed and transposed lives around them, with an exclamation, never to be felt again.

We never know from which corner of the universe God will enlighten us with His sounds and miracles, letting us experience His amazing grace. I was moved with an exuberant appreciation for the hard work the choir endured with tenacity and grit to deliver the fire they lit in each other and the people around them. Their love for music incited a determined push to move through adversities to overcome. Throughout their determination, it revealed to me that God is so faithful, He cannot fail. Roadblocks and diversion sometimes get in the way, causing us to war within ourselves. Without those obstacles, we could not master the appropriate tools to process and proclaim our purpose effectively.

God has in store for us so much more than we can ever imagine, think, or acknowledge. Our infinite minds are too shallow to see the bigger picture. As our king and savior, Jesus is Lord over all His kingdom. He is oh so faithful. He can never fail. As we move from Mount Sinai to Mount Zion, we are born into the deity of Christ, the living word of God the Father.

Thank you, George, an incredibly motivating young pastor from Heart of Worship Chapel in Reseda. Thank you for that meaningful message from the law of Moses to Christ, our redeemer, our strength, our healer, and our intercessor. Our hearing of the word and beliefs comes through our interpretation of God's thoughts. And, as they encounter and penetrate our heart, please be encouraged to receive graciously! The Lord says, "humility is a gift He gives us." When we give way to being humble, we can feel for others. We can understand pain, suffering, anger, poverty, rejection, and separation. Humility is attached to gratitude, mercy, faith, blessings, strength, love, and compassion. Our hearts are motivated to cry for others when we are humble. It is a powerful liberating feeling, a gift that encourages and changes lives, supports, and builds. Through our humility, God is present, standing right beside us, guiding us to be His helping hands, and expecting us to let go and let Him show us with an eager heart. He is so faithful,
He will not fail.

# Who are you affiliated with?

Check your account of affidavits and affiliations. As we leap into action and connect ourselves with various organizations, let's look at the significance of those with whom we affiliate. We trust, render obligations, obey multiple policies, regulations, and laws, and respect them without question. We choose to adhere to these ingredients according to the access we desire. Yet, as humans, we find it an actual challenge to observe and obey God's ordinances. We lend our confidence to human nature far more than giving credence to God's laws. We are reluctant to reach a consensus where God is concerned. But we will find ourselves going the distance, waving the flag of recognition for another human because we believe in what they sell us. Why is this? When I stand and listen to God's words and attempt to understand our attitudes, I find it unfortunate as to the conditions of our hearts. In paying attention to how Jesus lived His life, I am moved by His appreciation for the father's heart towards us. He gave us an example in His experience if we choose to pay attention. He was so obedient that He got baptized as a lesson for our future endeavors on planet earth! When are we going to realize that we are not created as a single entity but as a unit to serve and protect each other? Who are you affiliated with in your search for love, caution, trust, gratitude, respect, obedience?

Are you so entrenched in the cultural, legal entanglement of the human spirit you forget to take part in the creator's ordinance of a prosperous life? In 2 Kings, the prophet Elisha was obedient to the word and authority of God. His heart was in sync with the spirit and favors of God. He was a man directly affiliated with God. 2 Kings 5:11, Naaman's refusal to follow Elisha's directions and wash in the Jordan was beneath him. His affiliation was the spirit of man, unconnected to God's grace and mercy. It took a child, a young woman, to touch the heart of this self-prescribed man of authority to be obedient to God's word. "Simply dip in the Jordan seven times to be healed of leprosy." It was an uninspiring direction to his human self-centered obnoxiousness.

Are the things you are affiliated with more important than the soul you intend to save? Are we unconsciously aware of who we are affiliated with? It is not a philosophical question, just a natural perspective on the life we inhabit. Check your affiliation coat at the door of recognition.

# Sometimes we weep because we seek

In John 20:15, Jesus asks Mary, "Why are you weeping? Whom do you seek?" Sometimes we weep because we're disappointed, hurt, or discouraged. Sorrow has a way of entering our hearts when we're not ready to confront what we speak. Other times, weeping happens because we have received a revelation of joy. What we seek may bring encouragement, resentment, resistance, or reassurance to help others inspire as they deploy.

Jesus made it abundantly clear to Mary that her weeping is a natural reflection of seeking an answer to help her transpire. As Christians, we pray because we seek affirmation in our faith, like warring panthers. Do we understand that God's interventions will assuredly provide or produce a response? Undoubtedly, as we wait at His gate, He will reciprocate through our belief even when we ponder His wonder.

Jesus said to Mary, "as you weep, know that your seeking is not converted to clinging because your revelation is not in vain although you strain." I will ascend to the Father, a transformer for all who proclaim. He is my father, your father, the king of heaven, earth, and all that remains.

Assuredly, our trust is not a loss because we are ultimately sustained. His grace and mercy remain a staple in our weeping and seeking. His love will never refrain because He speaks to our hearts over and over again. So, as you weep and seek, remember to forgive, remain in peace, pray and know that God died so we will ultimately, beautifully, and abundantly survive to proclaim.

# Unlock your mental capacity

According to Mark 8:1-11, you may be locked up, but you are not locked out because God has the key to your gate, door, or corridor. You will gain fantastic insight beyond your brain's physical receptors. Once you're equipped with clarity, your reality becomes sharper, moving you toward your position in your reality. So intentionally glide to inspect your intentions. The entrance is within your grasp. God is bigger than anything you or I can ever imagine. It's within your preference or clasps.

It's up to us to see the possibilities in everything God has for you and me to understand. That was the question Jesus asked the disciples, "how much food do you have to feed the party of four thousand on the sand." They were incapable of looking beyond their circumstance. It was impossible to stretch their thinking that far in the distance.

A man without a vision is like a turtle without its protective resistance. It's like an architect without retrospect. Their future had no expansion into the abundance of the God they thought to understand. As humans, we must focus on what God has for us and seek to implement His direction. It's imperative and essential to reaching our destination, even with complications.

He has an incredible plan for your life and mine if we choose to be humble and realize the best is yet to come. I believe this: look, listen, and incorporate His construction without any deliberate objection.

# What is your cause? Acts 19

What is your cause as a Christian? What do you expect when you come into the spiritual and physical experience of God's uniqueness? Do you clearly understand?

Our attitudes and beliefs require a genuine understanding, a homogeneous relationship between faith and grace if the plan is to stand. Are we willing to put in the work with substance?

Amid challenges, are our hearts familiar through prayers to push pause if we find ourselves at a false start?

Do we enact grace, pivot, or call upon the Holy Spirit no matter our circumstance? Or do we simply fall apart?

As believers, how familiar are we with the Holy Spirit retrospectively? It's impossible to fail during our walk with Christ Jesus even when we fall because forgiveness was established on the cross; all is never at a loss.

It is impossible to be in Christ and not know the Holy Spirit because He dwells inside your heart. It is also imperative to grasp who God is inside and outside our souls; we are worth much more than silver and gold.

Paul's release of the holy spirit through baptism transpired a transformation of some, causing a riot and pushing others into a state of rebellion.  Instead, that conversion caused a multitude of conversations about Paul's message because we know that Christ is not dead.

Choices were established, setting a direction of accomplishments and putting our faith base in action. Paul's gospel preaching was an educational journey to the disciples' purpose. The introduction of Jesus was a new phenomenon that spanned two thousand centuries plus. Human hearts were made for alignment into completeness with Christ's, that's right.

He is not a ghost! So do not be afraid simply because He arose from the dead; he was not indisposed. Freedom comes from discarding false perceptions. Reject fear and lies and live in redemption.

It's a change of our convictions, a regeneration of our interpretation; a strengthening of our faith for our protection. Live in the spirit without fear; that sets us apart in God's grace, although there will be a provocation.

Our proclamation of independence empowers us to receive God's power; it's our salvation. He sends His advocates for our assistance. They show up as our helper, counselor, way maker, strengthener, encourager, and comforter.

He will never leave us or forsake us. He is our gatekeeper. Clarity, understanding, wisdom, and discernment are influencers over our consciousness; they are our heart's sweepers because lying is an outpouring of our unconscious emotions.

We are required to live in love, serve with patience, kindness, forgiveness, forbearance, and be a blessing of effective practices. With dedication, we grasp God's grace and prosper in the spirit of God's character. Otherwise, we are without patience, reverence, respect, integrity, or diligence. Our cause finds itself in its place; that's how we were wired.

So never get tired; we are created in His image and built to endure. Don't spend time speculating. Be bold, regulated, and impactful. Become God's ambassador. Even when we feel like amateurs, believe in the cause. It's a positive purpose as we walk through God's open doors.

# Your destination is a victory

God has purposely designed His plans for you. It's so easy to lament and destroy what you have a fear of building in a day or a year. Remain focused, committed, and constant in your dream to believe and thrive to stay alive. In your faith to carry on, see your journey without fault to follow through. Let your fight be as big as your dream and know that you cannot do anything alone.

For God to multiply himself, He had to die, which is the principle of creation. Sacrifice is the key to victory. Doing service for God is doing service for others. When you go before God, be present. Work from a victorious standpoint. Don't work towards victory. Once you are there, give Him praise, honor, and glory.

"My joy is to inspire my readers to move from promise to purpose in your land with intentions, integrity, love, honesty and liberty for your liberation."

# SISTERHOOD

## An unwelcomed intrusion to my womanhood

I felt as if I was being invaded by intruders from unknown planets; otherwise known as fibroids. My struggle, my journey with these unknown intruders began about six years ago. This metaphorical intrusion entered my private mansion, my space without invitation.

This burglar is unsettling in the life of a woman, especially a strong black woman. I was the unsuspecting recipient of this crippling kryptonite. Women are supposed to be the salt of the earth, the backbone of all that is a challenge. But sometimes we are confronted with obstacles or obstructions that can either make or break us.

I gave birth to six planets yesterday. One the size of Earth, one the size of the Sun, and the other sizes ranging from Pluto to Mars. I am relieved now. I can reboot, rebuild, restructure, and strengthen my mind as I fit the pieces of myself back together. Over the past six years of suffering from my planets, my life changed tremendously.

My journey mimicked a basket weaver struggling to create a sound basket out of damaged straw. It was frustrating as I tried to navigate work hours, and school hours, along with what felt like a withering social life. It left me with shortness of breath, periods of swelling, and times when I thought I would never stop bleeding. The monthly blows I experienced held me captive and pushed me sometimes to a place I would just collapse. This was a scenario of a bullying experience for me. But, let me say to you, there is nobody greater than God. I'm not sure if anyone else has ever gone through this period of devastation, a wilderness experience. It gives me the distinct resemblance of a tight hold on my inner parts. It is not an appealing or well-received rewarding experience.

Fibroids can cripple your desire to engage with the people you have relationships with. I had to decide. The day I reconciled to attack this uninvited guest; it was welcomed jubilation acknowledging that I wanted to take charge of my life once again. My doctor was very supportive of her knowledge and experience with this disruptive disassociation. I embraced the opportunity to chastise this invasion of my privacy.

I was a willing patient. Prayers, God's assistance, and a team of medical experts, and their professional experiences, conquered this taxing troll. Today I'm living with hope, unafraid to roll a troll. To every black woman suffering from their own planets, please give yourself permission to take back your life. Put fibromyalgia in its place and reject the notion that you are an essay of undefined, unfinished substance. Own your option to be celebrated and liberate your future. I commend you on your drive to be empowered. Dare to regain your tower of power. You are a wonder, a magnificent, brave warrior, never surrender.

To: My daughter Alex
From: Mom

# His obsession became a pre-occupation

He intentionally and deliberately positioned himself to meet his obsession.

It was an odd, mysterious situation.

A woman auditioned for a role and was drawn into a spiderweb of infliction.

He sought her as a way to quench his thirst for integration.

His perilous life reflects a trajectory of unpredictable behaviors of rejection.

He entered her life with poetry and insanity.

Without vicious intent, she played into his psychosis unknowingly.

They called in the fixer to destroy the evidence unequivocally

She did not report her mess-ups to the media universally.

The intervention was successful without a hitch during her dependency.

It was done with dutiful transparency.

# I ain't store-bought!

You can't paint me on a bottle and sell me in the store.

You can't put me on a shelf and put a price on me.

You can't label me unfit, for God has already ordained me to be.

You can't sell me in bulk. You can't weigh me like oranges for my pulp.

I ain't store-bought.

According to Galatians 3:15, Christ purchased my life with his blood on the cross.

You can't use my skin color against me or the coarseness of my hair to erase your fears. For God made me. Are you clear?

I ain't store-bought.

I cannot be returned or exchanged or recycled like broken glass.

 I am of purpose with fearless class.

Please remove the assumption of your self-righteous misguided attitude.

I am not the thing in the go-back bin.

Or the can on the shelf filled with candy for yourself. I am filled with hope. My happiness encompasses love and gratitude.

I ain't store-bought!

# Ladies, "here I am"

As a woman, I too believe in the power of love. It represents an amazing elixir of varying degrees. Love operates as a mixture of joy, trust, belief, empowerment, faith, fairness, transparency, integrity, a strength builder, communication receptor, a commitment influencer, gratitude inviter, courage carrier, blessings, and a center for God's grace. But there are times when the word love bears a heaviness, a different flavor of tears. The initiator ignites a sober blow of self-serving ego. The egotist inflicts an influence of distraction under the guise of love. It becomes cloudy, dark, painful, rejecting, abusive, physically and emotionally challenging. The influencer begins to act like a junior government official. Meaning they make the rules; they are the gatekeepers of your souls. They are in complete control of your destiny. The hidden encrypted language is "oppression." You are left without any bargaining power of your natural spirit. I say, "keep knocking" because one day the door will open.

Remain in faith, because behind every door lies your dreams and aspirations. So, you must keep knocking, working, pushing, engaging, committing, believing, and communicating. You have the power to open the doors to your destiny.

In Matthew 7:8, God vividly said, "For everyone who asks receives; he who seeks finds; and to him who knocks, the door will be opened." In this clear statement, our father is transparent with open arms. If you're looking for a man, look no further. His love is still simply this, "ladies, here I am, because I am the I am." You will find Him to be of comfort, wholesome encouragement, peace, prosperity, transparency, integrity, with proper equity in this place of grace.

In no way, shape or form am I installing a single framework of how to get a man. I'm only sharing with you that without the power of faith, it is impossible to relate within the context of what God has in store for your mate. So, ladies, keep knocking. Keep searching. Keep smiling and be blessed in your hope chest of encounters. God is on the throne with His arms wide open to impress and impart His love songs in your hearts without impartiality. As Bruno Mars shares, "ladies, if you're looking for a man, baby, here I am." Ladies, wait no longer for your man. He is sending the message of inclusion. His availability and access are your destination.

You are loved and deserve love inside and out. So, don't consider yourself counted out. Build your house and remain in the state of God's supernatural route. Ladies, He is shouting, "here I am. I am your man, without a doubt."

# Own you first

Listening to a report about the condition women often find themselves immersed in, struck me as eerily astonishing. I was profoundly moved by the gravity, a pull that evoked my spirit. I immediately sensed my emotions swaying in varied measures. As I quivered and quickly sprung from the trauma of pent-up feelings, a sadness aroused in me. As a woman, a woman of darker melanin, I'm perplexed about the reasons women indulge in relationships that wield no respect for their strength, vigor, dreams, or ambition. Corinthians 13:13 states, "And now these three remain faith, hope, and love. The greatest of these three is love." Love you first.

Sometimes it matters not your cultural background or level of financial reflection. Women sometimes choose men who represent inflamed cracked limbs. We sometimes embrace them, as if they are songs with a savory flavor of good essence. In fact, they are without balanced rhythms when it comes to us settling into relationships. I would like to interject a thought of acceptance that may disturb some of us women. God loves us regardless of how we see ourselves. It is paramount to give, share, and be loved because that's how we were created. We were created to connect with each other as humans.

We assume we can correct the flaws and slow the flow of the men who disregard our devotion to them. Women often do so by affirming men, by soothing what feels like magical, but imperfect nature. Unfortunately, it's the opposite. Women often become the broken ones, the song that stays on the recorder stripped of her meaningful melodies and values. I sometimes see women in perilous situations, reluctantly making choices to stay, leveling their ambitions, and self-esteem to the ground. These women are now alone. It may be because of the affluence they were accustomed to, or they have become accepting of the reality of their broken crown. But they are now trapped in a place where leaving is not an option. Their world is a threat, living in an upside-down frown. However, their souls are now estranged from the women they were meant to be. They are not free.

Women fondly showcase themselves without a thought as to who they are as individuals. The unfortunate influence you have connected yourselves to becomes the very thing that strangles you. It's like an epiploic appendage draining your vein, cutting off your ability to see clearly how to survive. You are now caught in a web of self-destructive. self-torching behaviors. The outward appearance you depended on has long lost its shelf-life appeal. Now you are left looking back at the mirror of regrets. Why is our society so trenched in the superficial skin complexities and physical aesthetics that eventually erode the integrity of a woman's true virtues? This complicates a woman's composition when the sense of self becomes a dismal rescue.

We will need to go back to the basics. I believe it is a necessary mental health exercise and application of retractable decisions to redefine your self-worth. It's time to re-enter our past histories of self-sabotaging behaviors and pursue a new birth. Reach back to our inner younger selves and carefully caress the beauty within as the women we once felt. Without such aspirations, we will continue damaging the beauty within ourselves.

Without the stamina to stand up, stand out, and own ourselves first, we are doomed. We live in a society where men are seen as the diamonds and women are looked at as coal, good to keep the fire warm with no other usefulness. As a mother of a brilliant young, gifted, and black daughter, it was my duty to develop in her a personality and a position reflecting the woman that raised her. She is a reference to her tomorrow reflecting a vision for other young women to mirror if they so choose. It's not always a child's choice; I am all too familiar with that scenario. Having worked with students that were drawn into various grids of vulnerable unexpected situations, I am fully aware of the circumstances they encountered daily. But, as women who have mastered the living space of planet earth, we have the God-given decrees to establish a platform to help young women grow and thrive.

Children are incredibly resilient humans, especially young women, to thrive in a society that detracts the soberness from life. It is up to us to teach self-respect and modalities that uplift instead of ones that delete. Love is a lost art in society. It is sometimes missing from the womb. It must be our privilege and responsibility to re-engage young people through early learning interactions in an effort to bring inclusion, love, and sensitivity to our communities. We must teach women, young and not so young, to own themselves first, before handing off the mantle of ownership to a man that has no interest in who they are as women.

I have so many strong, vibrant women in my life that I can call on without a doubt for advice. They are like soldiers in an army of problem solvers going through the process with me: Mama Hill, Robyn, my sister-in-law Rhina, my mom, my sisters Jennifer and Gillian, and my sisters in the Lord Debra and Donna. Additionally, sister Grace, Donna, Kim, Melita, Ms. O, my best friend Myrandia, Melinda, Shayatia, and especially my daughter Alex are with me in the fight. These women are my pillars of strength. It is our duty to put a positive position of sincere gratitude, hope, trust, and love in place to create bonds of lasting blessings for our children. As women of sensibility, we owe this to our younger sisters.

# Sisters

They are not always blood relations, but they are from the heart with purpose and intention. They are the women that we are connected to in more ways than one. Sisters, serve us on bad days and good ones. Sisters empower perspectives and our passions, intercept our indiscretions, and impact our directions. They become our resources in time of reflection. They help us see things retrospectively, even though we may want to go off course indirectly. They surround us when we want to surrender to shame. They carry and encourage us in times when our faith is strained. They become our cheerleaders.

Sisters pray with us, dream with us, and motivate us into action and purpose. Sisters are insightful even when our identity and focus can't be found. Especially when the enemy has us sitting like a lost kite waiting for the wind to lift us off the ground. They acknowledge us and help us turn around and rethink our humiliations as our smiles are turned into frowns. Sisters meet us right where we are. They help to strengthen our thoughts and restructure the belly when we melt down. They hold us accountable when we would rather stumble.

Though we may be apart, my sisters are always in the center of my heart. Sisters might not be perfect, but they are the perfect mix in times we fall apart. Sisters are the women who uplift us through life's battles, beauties, and sometimes betrayals. They help us breathe and restart. They instill security when we love with passion and find that love is sometimes in retraction.

Sisters are there through the struggles, trials, pain, and triumphs. They guide us as we revamp our emotions and get back in compliance. Sisters are important when the possible seems senseless. They help us reshape our thoughts to restart our hearts, even when we think it's endless. Sisters help us declare our strengths when we come to a hill that says let's end this. My sisters are the women who are there when our minds, bodies, and spirit feel like they can't co-exist. This might be a time when you're just in a pointless twist. They bring us back to a place of grace and remembrance that there is a God who is a living constant fountain, even in our unplanned prayer space.

# We strut that beat!

Hello to all my beautiful black women. Black women are strong and brilliant, designed to endure a myriad of emotional sways and experiential plays. It is with God's Grace and favor that when the waves of the sea tempt us, He steps in, cradles us and remakes us so divinely in His ways. Women of darker melanin develop the ability to refresh and reframe. Many look at us and wonder what makes us so incredibly complicated, compassionate, driven, sexy, yet vulnerable to the touch. Many of you might interject the notion that we are inaccessible, antisocial, and impolite. Others claim that we are disrespectful, irrational, or unreliable. To those extremes, you will find that we are firm in our pursuit to achieve, forgive, love, and invite, despite the taxing drive to hide our tremendous pride.

We will unapologetically protect our rights from being brushed aside. Yes, we are brave in the fight to keep family tight because slumbering creates defeat at any black women's gate. We must strut our feet to compete and support in stride the timing of our heart's beat at any rate. It's sometimes confusing to see us because it's hard to greet us. Let me assure you we are the daughters of kings and queens made from genuine historical societies of gold dust. We are brilliant, extraordinarily magnified—black women with a passion for swallowing our pride and walking with a purpose in our stride.

We are rich in our presence and hopeful as we build confidence to conceal the mountains you try to put in our path not to survive. Some may assert that we are tested on every single side but be assured and understand that we are vibrant in our prospects of prosperity. Don't be surprised.

You assumed we had to emulate your realm of wordy inflections to reflect and assimilate. In your rail of disparity, you bring no clarity. Let me remind your overblown egos that you challenged us to impress, re-energize, and realize that we are the giants in the desert of a divided and conquered land. With that notion in hand, we lift up, strut up, and walk to the beat of our drums wearing an invited inner smile while building our brand. We are not unambiguous or unambitious, the disenfranchised reckless grandstand of rejection. We are Black women proud and diverse in our melanin, intending to survive beyond your illogical concept of our ability and remain firm in our stability. Realize and recognize that we strut to the beat of a drum not everyone can repeat! So, move all your Karens and Darens; this is one drum beat you will never repeat.

# The flower that blossomed and bloomed

I am exceptionally grateful for so many things. My life in Christ is a bountiful journey of trials, tribulations, and triumphs. If anyone tells you a different story, it is a fabrication of their lack of wisdom, understanding, and knowledge of who God is. Sometimes you get derailed, and you tend not to wait. Your patience is tested and tried by an illness, losing a job, a child's health, children's disabilities, or disobedience. No matter the circumstances, your frustration sometimes carries the burden of owning a situation you would prefer to forget. But God is never late, never early. He is always on time.

My flower is an excellent example of the favor God has given to me. My daughter is a gift that her dad and I did not see coming. She was a quiet child, but a talker from a curious perspective. From an early age, she was exceptionally gifted with words. Her insight and awareness were sometimes puzzling to me. She showed a level of understanding regarding her surroundings that made me stop and center myself more than once. We were driving back from a staycation with her dad on one occasion. It was pouring rain, and in my haste to get back to the valley, I laid the pedal to the metal. Meaning I drove faster than average.

As the rain powered down, a small voice gently made its way to my earshot. My daughter simply asked, "mommy is it raining? I respectfully responded, with a twitter in my brain, reframing and asked a redundant question such as this one: "Alex, what were you doing? Were you sleeping that you could not see that it is raining?"

In that instance, she quickly replied, "I know it's raining mommy. So why are you driving so fast?"

That moment blew my brain at her level of intentions and intelligence. She was probably four or five at the time. To see her quest to thrive by pushing the envelope on every side with a monumental glide and stride, told me that God was assuredly on her side. She forged through no matter the challenges she faced, even after having to undergo many medical procedures and a near-death experience. To see the magnitude of her strength in her perseverance, her inspiration in that episode in the hospital was to witness a woman whose spirit was connected to God and her mother. During a testing time when she should have been exhibiting concern, my daughter wanted to get her textbook and study while lying in the emergency room. This is the true spirit of having GRIT to me. That's the kind of tenacity and fierceness she wields.

On the upside of that, prayers and subjugation were being lifted to God's throne on her behalf by me and so many others. It is a personal petition between you and the Father as to the level of your faith over the fear you possess. Keep hope at the forefront of everything you experience in any situation. He is listening, and He hears your heart. I have discovered that determination is the prayer that God wants to put in our hearts before anything else. Be at peace and know without the shadow of a doubt that He is working out a positive outcome for your situation, no matter what it looks like or feels like.

At times, we unintentionally lose insight into what He wants for us. So, giving up is not an option before we even try. For me, trying is the first step to doing. The T-stands for touch; the R-stands for repeat, and the Y-stands for yet again. So never give in to situations that want to penetrate and slay you. Acknowledging that you're not strong is a positive road to healing; because God sees and understands who you are, and what you're going through. He understands what you need before you recognize your own need. He will provide, He will lift you up, but He needs you to be courageous and know that He is a provider no matter your circumstance.

My daughter lives that theory and practices every day. Her courageous spirit sent me back to school when she went back to earn her master's degree in organizational management and leadership. Her determination, drive, consistency, and resiliency took her to heights I did not dream of or expect her to reach. But again, she is a magnificent, beautiful flower to be reckoned with. She returned to school, earned a second master's in psychology, while studying and passing the boards to become a board-certified behavior analyst. She is strong in her beliefs and is unstoppable in her position to succeed.

She is a bonafide achiever. She works with willing hands. Proverbs 31:13-14 says, "She is like the ships of the merchant; she brings her food from afar."

I thank God for her infectious staying power. Today she has earned the right to be called Doctor Alexandria Washington, with a Doctor of Psychology. She is a dog mom to Harper, and a living, loving, blossoming partner with Martin. "The heart of her husband trusts in her and he will have no lack of gain." "She is far more precious than jewels." (Proverbs 31:11)

Blessings are the unseen raindrops from God, and I have been showered with them through my daughter's journey. Myths are told every day to young black children in a country that calls herself a cradle for those that are cast with a clouded past. Her sentiments are inscribed on the Statue of Liberty: a gift from the people of France. She has watched over New York Harbor since 1886, and on her base is a tablet inscribed with words penned by Emma Lazarus in (1883): "Give me your tired, your poor, your huddled masses yearning to breathe free".

The word on the streets of this complex social mix of insecurities, lies and fears, tells women of various backgrounds and economic status that they and black women cannot coexist in the same communities because of the lack of faith, beliefs and trust of people in our society. Black women must outshine, out master in everything they do, say, and portray if they desire to prosper. It's never too late, or impossible to correct a wrong.

I have seen Alex, growing up as an only child, create a myriad of relationships because she was able to amalgamate her environment and enrich her circle of engagements with other women outside of her immediate surroundings. My daughter is well rounded, gifted and a diversely fashioned woman. She is my beautiful Shero! She is the flower we planted, blossomed and bloomed. "Nothing is impossible that God cannot fix, do, or solve; it does not exist," are words from a song that strengthens my soul. And I sincerely hope it brings peace to you when you can't see the promise or possibilities. To me, Alex is that promise and possibility. The flower that bloomed reflects the delicate petals from my heart to yours, and from her heart to every young woman who wishes to blossom and bloom.

# The loneliness of a coveted wife

It may have the looks of a privileged world, living life on a two-edged sword. It's marvelous to have friends who see you as the prize wife. Some may romanticize looking into the face of the wife with all the right moves and just the right material supplies. These material impracticalities are the standard in a world of pretense. Your perfect ideal environment is the talk of the town. Secrets are percolating, permeating the air, but no one wants to confront all the frowns and snares. Nor do they wish to confirm the apparent conflicts looming in the background, like loose spare tires. The men hide in the shadows of life's challenges, all the while suffering from deep depression emerging like wildfires.

On the surface, things are joyous, happy, and shallow commitments run deep like undercurrents. Life experiences are filled with extraordinary and unexpected situations, especially when the pain constantly reminds you of the storms in the backyard not yet confronted. The cheating game is uncontested, and trust gets broken. Unspoken behaviors igniting the fires that kindle infidelity, financial improprieties, loveless, and empty unemotional support that disrupt marriages. The closet of unpredictability opens into psychological imperfections. Yet, we would rather disregard the truth revealed, and leave past histories of recklessness as a paper-thin memory carried like a baby in a carriage.

Sometimes a wife can feel the scales of the unbalanced weight, and it becomes an unbearable burden to carry. So, she can't relate. Until a light is brightly shown and all covered secrets revealed to be examined and rated. The outward appearance is a sham, cloaked with physical aggression, and male testosterone is vividly acknowledged in this realm. Relationships are strained, feelings are displayed, although the playful distractions avail them. In some cases, serious issues are shared between friends, and one can quickly leave the well-intended purpose of a faithful closeness to upend. The blow-up is about to ensue, where dirty laundry is hung for the entire community to view. Nerves are now raw and on edge.

The vulnerabilities are painted red on the wall of deception. All the secrets are unveiled, and the well of unprecedented details are told. Friendships will never look, feel, or live on the same road ever again.

So, when you come across a wife that appears to have it all, remember, we are all humans filled with vulnerability and imperfection. We can fall; not everything is a gem. But always remember that God is the creator of all, and He covers every tenant of who we are, the good, bad, and the indifference. Never judge a book by its cover without reading its content before making that judgment; you will forever need a page to reference. The loneliness of a coveted wife can sometimes mirror outward perfection. She may suffer from unseen rejection. As humans, we are flawed, but knowing how to forgive is a powerful tool that brings us closer to withdrawing our claws.

FYI: Remember to stay alert to those who surround you. While they seem to stand with you on common ground, be aware because everyone has flaws.

# This world is your canvas

We are magnificent wonders, giving one opportunity to go round on this beautiful planet. It is entirely according to your perspective of the entitlement you allow yourself. The world is your oyster, show up and represent. Take the events of your journey and use them as a painter who leaves an account for the world to take notice of. Not because you wish to boast, but because it is your responsibility to change someone's vision for their future. In 1 Peter 4:10, the bible says: "As each has received a gift, use it to serve one another, as good stewards of God's varied grace." By painting today's picture, let it be of sincerity, stability, wisdom, love, and transparency.

We are the best and the worst of God's design. Some will choose to be inventors, investors, innovators, instructors, information realtors, engineers, inspirers, ingenuity creators, increasers, insightful attitudes carriers, or insurance preparers.

Others will instead incorporate individual dependence, increased indulgence, and invasive treatment of other, indignant, insecure, and irrational souls. The impact they render is that of negativity insurers. Their lives are riddled with insults on the rights of others, igniting ferocious infractions on those they believe to be illegal, illiterate, or imbalanced imbeciles.

As you participate in life's experiences, put your engagements to purpose. Learn to incorporate the brush strokes of the pictures you create to encourage others that the world can be a different story for them. Take in every morning, midday, afternoon, and evening, as a new adventure. Remember, nothing stays the same. The things you did this morning might not be the same tomorrow morning, with the exception of God shining His face, giving you the grace to take a breath one more time. Jeremiah 29:11 says, "For I know the plans I have for you, declares the Lord, plans for welfare and not for evil, to give you a future and a hope."

Validate who you are as you awake daily, spared from the grave of gravel. Be in gratitude as you pick up the paintbrush with a smile and strike a line of faith, hope, resilience, respect, progress, and prosperity in your recovery. Recognize the light of life and paint with dignity. As you retrospect on your relationships, remember that responsibility plays an enormous role in the picture or pictures you paint and leave for others to encounter, enjoy, reject, or regret.

Your movements will encourage the footprints as someone else's roadmap to navigate. Your actions are today's accounts for your children and their children. So, with every stroke you take in this life, let it be a piece of the puzzle for others to collect and cultivate. Let it be a bridge to help someone else pick up the easel and cross into their artistic endeavors. Paint pictures so vivid in a world where others are desperate to erase your thoughts, imagination, integrity, and courageous spirit. Today sets the tone for a tomorrow we may not be around to inspire, unless you leave a message in your paintings to transpire. Your today is someone's tomorrow of thanksgiving with gratitude. I pray they will have a fearless attitude as enquirers, because the world will be their canvas to paint and reach higher.

# I know a Shero

She is beautiful and vibrant. A dreamer of a sorts, strong, intentional, tremendously brave, and the embodiment of grace to everyone she meets. She is a monument to her community, and a golden nugget, yes, to each child she encounters. She delights in giving and receiving sincere hugs of gratitude.

Her vision stretches way beyond borders from generation to generation. She is the heart and soul of the people she touches. She serves as a role model to those who need encouragement.

She is a brilliant and a bright light to all the befuddled sockets around her. Her desire to enlighten a difficult moment for others is to bring focus, allowing those she touches to open their eyes to see the glory that surrounds their possibilities. She is wise in her thoughts. Her actions can be traced to her outstretched arms. Her open heart reveals a vessel to impart education, wisdom, love, knowledge, and inspiration, generating life lessons to embrace achievements in a positive essential learning environment.

Her motive is simply relational in creating community engagement to change a negative situation by empowering a movement of natural success. Her ability to bring groups of various people of different classes together produces the kind of transparency pairing with the essential essence of growth. She is a wonder; her insight is nothing short of relentless passion shared by her love for all living humans.

She opened her personal doors to encompass trust, the admittance of open minds, self-control, and selflessness, raising self-esteem, and lifting the foundation to restructure broken spirits. Her efforts of loyalty to transform a frayed and frightened group of young people into a place of promise are vital to their self-awareness. She activates minds to open and build new generational relationships as they move forward with a message of hope.

She began her work journey on a road that needed elevation, paving the way from a condition of unattainable future for many. She paid attention to making a difference and changed the attitude of turning wrong thoughts into right thinking mindsets; knowing that was the only thing to do. The good news is that she is unmatched in her relentless pursuits to give back to those who should be counted as unworthy.

My admiration for her tender heart is unfathomable because her fight is of faith, warmth, love, care, passion, and confidence. She is magnificent in her unwillingness to give up on anyone, or projects she embarks on. I can't wait to see this amazing woman emerge from a valiant place of hard work to a majestic queen of grace for the work she continues to do in her commitment to changing her community's future, one child at a time.

My shero is my Mama Hill.

# GRATITUDE

## Beach day

Beach day, Tuesday morning, sprang as if I was on a duty call to a military action alert. I was awakened to my alarm clock ringing like I had been summoned to roll call at 6:30 AM. We took to the partially congested 101 like gravel to cement. We arrived at the sounds of the ocean's water rushing like thunder, flowing straight from an unknown source. Yes, we surrendered. Oh, but this source was tangible, touching my being like a blast of pure warmth running through me. Birds and people are mesmerized by its grace, beauty, and terror all at the same time. I am grateful to be in the awesomeness of a paradise designed to uplift and tantalize my senses. My dear friend Kim and I set out on a journey to escape and capture a different kind of day from the usual mundane trafficking we face in the valley of the San Fernando Basin.

As we continued our day-out, we finally engaged in a somewhat chilly but magnificent view of the rumbling water, we were impressed. The experience lifted my spirit from its dull drum state. It was a very picturesque vision, as if seeing the ocean for the first time. We had not gazed at its beauty during the COVID-19 isolation. Now it had a different appearance. We were vulnerable to its grasp and set out to imperfectly take as many photoshoots as if we had never experienced the mind-boggling sweet aroma of sea salt in our entire lives. The formations of large and small groups of rocks caught my attention as they stood out like monuments with birds attached to them. Some were so profound that they gave the impression of mountains subdued by the waves crashing alongside their walls. It was breathtaking!

After snacking on an aromatic mouth-watering fruit salad made by my friend, I ventured into the water, along with a delicious wrap from my favorite market. I launched and slowly submerged my weary, tired feet in the ocean with a wide grin and determination. I intended to touch the water's edge of the swelling ocean as it raced back and forth. But instead, my left slipper decided it too wanted to experience that salty flavor of the sea. It left my foot without proper warning and took off, not requesting my permission.

Laughter became my release of what appeared to be a kidnapping situation by the waves and the tugging sand that grabbed my slippers. I was astonished to watch my shoe float away right before my eyes. So, I temporarily lost my sanity and flung the other shoe to find its mate. I laughingly headed back to our spot on the sand and tried to explain the unbelievable scenario to my friend Kim. To which she burst into a hysterical chuckle.

Interestingly enough, I was delighted with the outcome of not having to wear shoes home. I quickly realized it was not the best decision made as the weather grew smoldering with the heat as the morning wore on. And by the time we left, my feet were under extreme pressure to find something other than what felt like hot lava mixed with sand accompanying each step I took. The journey back to the car was like working with a spy camera, detecting ways around the burning fragments under my now two wobbly fringed drumsticks. It was a beautiful reunion between myself and my chariot, as referred to by Kim. I had the most amazing time watching the ocean do her thing. However, I want to encourage everyone who finds the beach to be their thing, to take a pilgrim passage to your favorite beach spot and live like it's your last day.

It was mesmerizing, awe-inspiring, soul cleansing, and well worth the trip with my good friend. My dear friends, the moral of the piece is never forget to love yourself in the process of living.

# Love ambushed and trapped her almost to death

The love she sought kept her hiding in the dark. It was now the cause of what made her fight to save her own life. Her search for self was mind-blowing and was now on pause.

Be careful what we pray for! The saying "I need to get married and have a man," is an essential manuscript in the expectation of so many women's hope chests. So, we put our hearts, faith, trust, and request out to the universe, so to speak. The notion that it's important to be a wife is rooted in the optionless tradition of society. Women, including myself, often ask God to send us the man of our dreams.

The request goes like this; he must be tall, dark, and handsome for other women to glare with envy. Then comes a sister-like friend who says, "I have the perfect man for you. He will be the silver lining in your moonbeam with no strings attached."

"Wow, I must meet this guy!" she touted. "He will treat me like a queen, and protect me from the storm, and give me the world." So, she relaxed her reality.

We live to meet the man of our dreams, right? Then unfortunately the wolf sheepishly strolls in sheep's clothing. He is mesmerizing and charming. His eyes are devilish, but she likes them and becomes enticed. It was just what she needed to quench her thirst of being single and alone, tired of the moaning and agonizing.

My Mr. Right came to rescue me from my pain of insecurities. He was going to set me up on his throne. I would never be alone. It was love and romance like I had never known. He wooed me and fine-dined me. With wine and expensive trinkets, he enshrined me. He made me feel like I was the only thing in his mad, mad world. Although I saw the signs, I rejected the thought, because we were in flow. He was working to uproot my heart. He sold my soul to bury me in a plot I didn't secure. The abundance became the abuse dance. Regularly, I was assured, not paying attention, that I was insecure.

I worked hard to uplift my life educationally, socially, and professionally. I am now being subserviently measured. My faithfulness was now a curse instead of a blessing to the marriage I saw and treasured. I gave it my all, pulled out all the stops, while others saw my bravery as something crazy. Instead, my personal life felt like mental and physical slavery in his hands of dependency. Was I still on board with this calamity? My family and some close friends relinquished my soul in selfish traditional values and gave their blessings because I was counted as gold.

The deceit ran deep; love worked against me in defeat, making me vulnerable and incomplete. I am now lost and sold. At times, I didn't understand. What makes this idiot so cold? He is harmful even to the sole of my feet? I tell my story of life's disasters, this emotionless cobweb I'm entangled with in these streets. It's a dangerous, rhythmless mentality. Hate had become my reality. Some people are sympathetic, and others are still living in philosophical complacency. He took my voice, suffocated my spirit, and trod on my convictions. I am like pressed grapes ready for compost; destruction is my destiny. Is there no compensation? I have been tried on every side, with crushed dreams and bliss-less marital pride.

I met with soothsayers from my tradition. They spoke with forked tongues. Everything was for their gain. I believed God had left me to die without cause and in vain. Was this a plan? Who was I to complain? All the while, my fairy tale life was being shredded as I stood and breathed. Prayers seemed to cause the demons to register sharp blows. I'm stunned each time I encounter pain. I ask, is this my burial wreath? But I kept believing that it's something I was doing wrong. Yet there is hope among the thorn, an Angel that God put in my path; she's the sister that stands.

This angel encourages hope; her vote and prayers keep me afloat. She helps build my strength to fight for my right to thrive. My life is worth fighting for to stay woke. It is no joke. She stuck with me through thick and thin in this misery of abuse and infringement of my integrity, spirituality, and physicality. She carried me through my emotional boundaries. But God had my back when He sent another Angel in my path when I almost lost my child. Sometimes we can't see what he sees, and I want every woman to know you are one of his children. My life is now on the brink of recovery. He heard my prayers and touched my tears. He is the undoer of regrets and fears. It's time to reset my heart's clock. God has removed me from this madness and death trap. A woman must never allow anyone to infringe on her right to thrive. Love is what God has already prescribed.

You are loved, even if you think you're untapped. It's time to snap back.

# Love's confidence

The test of true love comes through one channel—the channel of obedience. No person should experience love as a burden, an entanglement, or an unfortunate incident. Couples find immeasurable connections when adversities destroy their faith, trust, and commitment. In this time, open your hearts and let God direct your path. It's the only proper course of action to strengthen your walk-in life with dignity, inclusion, and rejecting selfish ambitions. Love will remain constant when you use compromise as leverage to find your strength, as you declare courage over contention. He will enclose a solution to bring you through with confidence, no matter the situation or conflicts before you. In His own words, God tells us that the people of Israel were to Him, "as valuable rare gemstones set in gold." (Malachi 3:16-17 and Zechariah 9:16) Never be afraid to shine like the jewel God created you to be. Love is embracing your "Faith" even when you don't understand the complexities of your situation. His desire for us is to prosper.

Gods got you!

# Not today

*"Not today" is a song God put in my heart on a day that wanted
to bend and slay me.*

I know a man. His name is Jesus.
I woke up today on a Wednesday,
a morning with struggles on my mind,
a struggle I could hardly define.
I woke up with darkness in my head.
He came to me and said not today.
Struggles are not gonna perplex you in no way.
I know a man called Jesus.
He came and set me free.
I know a man called Jesus.
He came to deliver me.
When I was down and drowning,
He came and rescued me.
I know a man called Jesus.
He is who died for me.
I once tried to plan my pride,
He encouraged me to step aside.
His powers and love have no end,
Nothing is impossible for him to revive and mend.
I know a man called Jesus
He is my rose of Sharon on every side
I know a man called Jesus.
He came back to life to make me whole, so I glide.
Yes, I know a man called Jesus.
He lives in the very depths of my soul.
Yes, I know a man called Jesus,
we should all recognize,
Because this is a man that specializes.
Yes. I know a man called Jesus
Come on y'all and get baptized.
I know a man called Jesus.
He is my morning glory,
Yes, I know a man called Jesus.

He knows all of our stories.
Yes, I know a man called Jesus.
He is perfect in every way.
He will slay any temptation,
and say not today!

# One's attitude is everything

When you find yourself in a competitive compromising situation, leave the sound of fear behind. Enjoy one of the most spectacular moments of life in this magnificent time defined.

Be as salacious and independent as you can be.

Regret is not an option in the middle of life's strife because it can sting like a bee.

Your independence should never be clouded by fear because you are now free.

Never allow somebody else to dictate your worth, value, or belief so drastically.

Your happiness is unexplainable or pleasantly pleasing, depending on the interpretation of your reality.

Love should be simple, not reduced as an unintended consequence of someone else's random insecurities.

Their rebellious behavior is a rejection and a reflection of their given hesitancy.

A shared casual experience, if only for a day, is to be enjoyed as a lasting friendship of expectancy.

Time should not be laced or lost in jealous inhibition or disrespectful, restless, compromised tendencies.

Life's battles can force us into darkness or persuade and propel us into perplexing dependencies.

I say choose to live it out loud, enjoying every moment without regrets. Don't let missed intentions cloud your vision of happiness.

Create memories that will surpass every mind-blowing threat.

Instead, walk in exotic lustiness because love can meet you anywhere, even somewhere between a cold sweat.

One's attitude is everything; it's as simple as this.

Live out loud and shout; it's time to reset.

# A letter to mom

Dear mom,

As Mother's Day draws near, children young and not so young are sending their blessings and gratitude to the mothers who have loved and nurtured them. We are all so different as daughters. We have been blessed to have a mom like you. There is no doubt that you are one of a kind. A country like no other. You left your family and traveled to the UK, to expand your life, to marry the man you love and believed in.

Thank you, mom for the examples you gave us as women. As your eldest daughter, I am grateful for your courage to triumph through adversities. You're strong in grace and mercy, and that inspires me to keep my focus on the things that matter most: love for my siblings, my daughter, and others around me.

You show me to never stop dreaming, no matter how challenging the path might get. You took risks that your siblings did not dare to take, at such a tender age. You had a desire to seek a better life for your family and you bravely forged the course. Once again, you sojourned without looking back.

You stretched your wings and flew. You touched down on the ground of your destination, the U.S., in a place called New Jersey. The mountains you encountered could have set you back, but you leveled them into roads, which made it easier for your children to walk.

Your vision for us to succeed grew from the encouragement you received from Papa Allen. You trailblazed your way, which became our destiny, therefore creating a legacy. You shepherded us when unpleasant times wanted to prove otherwise. You kept your faith, held steadfastly to your belief, and steadied yourself in God's hands according to God's plan. I love you for the amazing journey you blazed for me. A light that will always shine as the world can sometimes get dim.

You are a warrior in every way one can imagine, and without hesitation designed a roadmap for your children to follow. I will continue to share these lessons with my daughter. I could not have asked God for a better example to draw from. You are a woman of introspection that I absolutely respect.

Your daughter Mer.
I love you in Jesus' Name.

# Don't get her wrong

My mom is not your typical mom; she is an extraordinary woman, insightful and duty-bound to her children.

She may give it to you in shotgun style, but you can never dismiss her effort in her delivery, for she is versatile.

Her overzealous attitude paints a picture of roughness sometimes that can appear unsympathetic. But I get it.

Her unconventional courageousness on the outside disguises her softness on the inside.

Don't get me wrong if you don't know her, you won't understand.

She is regal in her stance that whenever she exerts that confidence and strikes that iron; she strikes it with a force maintaining her convictions.

That in itself gives her children reason to belong, and I love her for that even through our contentions.

I love you, my dear mom, in every sense of the word. Your determination will always say stay strong!

# Obligated for life

There is a saying that goes something like this, "blood is thicker than water." What exactly does that mean, I asked? So, I researched its meaning and found that it may have originated from a German author, Heinrich der Glîchezære, in 1180. It may also be from the supposed original proverb, "The blood of the covenant is thicker than the water of the womb." (mystudentcvoices.com)

It simply implies that a relationship with the womb is stronger than that of an outside contender. We are born in families where sibling rivalry is familiar to a serious problem, right? But there comes a time, perhaps a place, where lives are threatened, and in this situation, one sibling must make sacrifices to protect the other. Within that environment, decisions will at times separate the physical but never emotional boundaries between them. It may appear to others on the outside that the circumstances or behaviors were obvious and must be dealt with accordingly through appropriate and effective accountability. But, unless you are directly involved in the cause of the external damage or consequences, your case is now, as we say in Jamaica, "Awash!" (unsubstantiated).

This story is about two children of the same mother but two different fathers. One is the daughter of a wealthy diamond distributor. The other is the daughter of a close friend of the mother. The girls did not know that they were from two very different backgrounds. Their mother suddenly died, and the father became confused, disoriented, and disillusioned about how to move forward. In other words, he gave up after the death of his beloved wife. The girls depended on each other for everything. The elder became the caretaker of her younger sister (DK), short for Danica Kristian. They did everything together. The elder (JK), Jenesis Kristian, left school early to support her sister's aspirations. DK had dreams of becoming a world concert opera singer. Her older sister worked to help DK achieve her dream. She began voice lessons at JK's former music teacher's home. DK began studying at the ripe old age of three and spent every waking hour practicing. One day, a friend of her older sister stopped by to drop off a package and became enthralled by her musical skills. He was fascinated with her beautiful green eyes and mellow-yellow complexion. His enthusiasm got the best of his reality on a dark, rainy Saturday evening. He did the unforgivable, the unthinkable; he attempted to deflower her and was killed.

Needless to say, the story takes a darker turn. The small town's law enforcement was meticulously active in the various scenarios sputtering around the town of Misgivings, Maine. DK was only thirteen at the time. She had developed a strong bond with her older sister and followed her every move. JK kept a small handgun under the magnetic countertop in the kitchen she had built. The peace of perils was her name for it. She kept it for protection, just in case of a situation such as this. One day, JK was in the basement cleaning up for a party planned to celebrate DK's opening event at the city center stage, a small musical theater in town. She heard a gunshot and rushed upstairs to find Ish lying in a pool of blood. She immediately took the gun from DK's hand and held it as if she had committed the crime. Her decision to protect her younger sister was as natural as the air they breathed. This acknowledgment left her with a criminal history and a twenty-five-year separation from her sister's dark reality.

DK became a part of the foster care system but continued pursuing her dream living with bits and pieces of those piercing memories, and tortured experiences. She lived in a world that attempted to protect her from her only sister, who was now stigmatized by her surroundings with negative attitudes from the community in which they grew up. Who would believe that the familiar faces and places around her showed a distant disgrace of heaviness and an emptiness as vivid as the forest floor? Over time, DK would experience the forces of her ancestors' power from the grave, urging her to seek revenge on the people who had put her sister away. As DK quietly mourned her sister's suffering, she would experience sinister forces taking her down macabre corridors. These scary thoughts exported her back to the place of the murder twenty-six years earlier. She would often move from town to town, trying to escape the recurring dreams with bits and pieces of flashbacks, but never a full episode of the trauma that changed her life. The more her therapist Julia attempted to uncover her past, the more frightened she became. Until one day, as she sat in the very chair where she last saw her sister's face, a small shadow confronted her memory. A front porch visit, and a cloudy stranger, took her vividly back to that forgotten, cold, wet rainy night.

The stranger was her older sister's father, the diamond distributor, whom she had never met. He read the story and tracked the girls down through a private investigator. At least those were the memories she struggled with. She lived alone in her darkness, although there were people she cared about in her life. It took her back down memory lane, and she recalled and recaptured the entire events of that lost memory that she chose to block out. The unfortunate reality was that JK was too weak to travel. She could not accompany her to any of her upcoming engagements. The town's mentality was that her sister was a murderer and deserved to be treated with disdain, rejection, and malicious behavior.

DK visited her older sister on a warm sunny Saturday afternoon. She took JK's hands and held them to her chest to remind her of the day she saved her life. In this space and time, she gave the grandest concert to a crowd of twenty thousand people in the UK's town square theatre. She executed her clout, using money deposited in her bank account from an unknown source to plan for JK to join her in the UK. Never underestimate the power of the blood that flows through the veins of siblings; because it will always run deeper and thicker than any stranger can ever imagine. The tiny town of Unforgiving, Maine, will never know the true story of the events that shook the town's core twenty-six years earlier. Even in those moments when you are tested to the core, always remember; that there's an open door. "You are never alone," saith the Lord. "I will go before you; I will never leave or forsake you."

# The bitter sweetness of sisterhood

L ove is the true test that reflects the vulnerability and valuable treasures of the heart. Sisters are the product of an unavoidable relationship, formed from love in the womb. It begins between a mother and a father's seed. These rivalries play a pivotal role in the sustainability of the bond between them through trials and triumphs. The effervescent effects of how a family interweaves begins from the foundation of how we are illuminated in our present. Our words, actions, and interplays are the living examples we present to our children as references. From this, they freely draw their examples, leading to the road of life's perspectives. Your training may incorporate ways to dispense forgiveness or revenge. Either way, it's your blueprint they draw from.

Sibling rivalry can be a dangerous game between sisters, even in transport. Sometimes secrets play a decisive role in the integrity of the relationship. In that circumstance, the possibilities can definitely cut a wedge between these bonds as they become unstable souls. Sistership depends on that strong bridge. It's the connection to help heal a sensitive situation. Selfishness is not a prescription for an unconscious person to elicit under any condition. Generosity goes a long way when we can reevaluate our conditions in its present circumstance. If the core values are blurred, it will therefore deny our egos any irrational thoughts. We must strive to be transparent. It is in moments like these we attempt to control our dignity. No matter what ignited the problem in the first place, reengage so that you can prevent a renegade. The bitter sweetness in sisters is not an uncommon example. When positive reflections are transparent, you can handle with a spindle. Your love should be the staple that binds and motivates your connection of confidence as an unbreakable sample.

CULTURE

# CULTURE

## Buried freedom will translate into life's disruption

Do not be fooled by your own hidden agendas in raising your man child, or woman child. Allow a certain capacity for growth to help shape their future by fertilizing their base with rich opportunities. Opportunities that will populate a strong seed of self-confidence. I thought I was liberated but then realized I was incorporated into a system of penal consequences.

Don't take them for granted. You will encounter sharper pitfalls, bombshells, resentment, and shadowy flashes when you least expect them. When we lose sight of their ability to think for themselves, we stifle their originality and influence potential disasters. There is no durability. Buried freedom fuels misguided judgments. It is imperative that we get as many real-life experiences as possible into our children's toolbox before they encounter the real-world trenches.

My unpretentious confidence determined my actions in a single moment of my life. I have recently been introduced to madness via the juvenile justice system. It was the lack of confidence in conquering my fears that led to a fractured spirit within me. I was an accomplice to my own demise. This was a far more complicated journey than I could have ever realized, way beyond my young, intrigued, uninterpreted mind. I have injured my intentions, my intellect, and my ability to control my impulse.

This is such a complicated moment even for me to grasp. I thought I was on top of my game, keeping everyone in the dark about my fears. Yet, I felt so frantically out of sync with my consciousness. I was so confused, yet no one realized. I was uncertain, and it felt like I could not prevent the inevitable. The day my reality came crashing to a dreaded frantic checkpoint.

To whom do I really belong raced through my mind. I asked myself, "where do I connect this distant yearning of unresolved questions?" My journey felt like chafed winds searching, reaching, and trying to figure out this pressing emptiness. Is it possible that I'm right where I need to be? Yet I keep trying to understand to whom and where do I belong? Or maybe I was just dead wrong.

I am intelligent. I am fierce and on so many levels I'm on top of my grades. But underneath it all, I struggle because I am frightened by the very things that keep me bound from the truth. I am an immigrant, I am a daughter, and I am a family member with secrets. I am related to greatness. Yet the fears I encounter lead me to retreat and make the wrong choices. Yes, I know where I can find love, but it too eludes me in moments like this. I often wondered if I will ever have a true understanding of the terrors that tremble within my soul.

I'm vexed, perplexed with questions that may never get answered. I sometimes get too involved in my own thoughts. Am I free to love, or am I really free to be loved? Will someone hear me outside of myself? I know some things I do are not in my best interest, but they seem to satisfy my curiosity. I'm not judged when I'm in this zone. In this space, I'm invincible. This Is Me. I tell myself to disquiet my torment. No one can overthrow me in my attraction to disappointment. I am powerful here in my faults.

Who can understand this unstoppable moment I so generously shared with myself? Does anyone out there hear me when I cry for help? Today I was caught, and I am still unclear why the deceit seems strange to everyone around me. I stole and continued to lie, as though this was the right thing to do. My whole life dangled in the balance, and I'm awkwardly thinking about how my friend was not getting something she needed.

I thought that I was someone who needed to save her from drowning. Instead, I was the one being dropped to the bottom of the pool. of a stinking mess. A residue of drowsiness swept over me. I was left with the sinking feeling of how am I going to address this regret. In this instance my life was in a complete state of unprecedented, perplexing tests. I was the one drowning in my own buried freedom.

How can I trust that the very thing I declared to do as right was going to detach me from a world that seems so clear to my family? I was loved but believed that I was not deserving of it. Now I'm further bound by the consequences I brought on myself, still I am astounded. I am now required to experience what it's like to have not. Tomorrow, I am now left to deal with a whole new set of traumatic circumstances.

I further realized that the reporting was really good for both me and my mom. We are now locked into repairing a past I thought I left behind as a child. But I have found that without, and within. God is bigger than anything, anyone, any trouble, or any ground I might find myself on. He is my Shepherd, my shield, and where I stand right now is not where I belong. For I know that He has my breakthrough. Satan tempted me into thinking that God was not on my side. The realization I was confronted with opened my eyes to the damage that potentially stood in my way. It would have threatened my life and future had I not connected my spirit to the brokenness I have within my very own life.

When low self-esteem overshadows our esteem, we are bound to spill and leak into our present situation. Learning to be accepting of the multiple ways God extends grace to us each day helps us survive crises that life experiences bring. We are better able to abandon any pseudo-philosophy we may want to hold dearly. I'm unsure what the future holds for me, because I'm still in my young state, hoping that God's generosity will continue to flow and cover me from day to day. I hope that I will someday forgive myself, the same way God has offered me freedom from self-doubt and learn to rely on His grace instead of relying on the educational system to declare my sense of direction through science. I will learn to release my freedom buried far too deep for too many years.

I am free to live, laugh, and love without selling my soul for a price. Because I still struggle with how to love myself. The underlying rebellion in my actions determined the mutated belief that my misguided behavior was simply that, unpretentious behavior. This place I'm in serves as a painful experience, never moving to a level beyond what it is currently. This was just a little crazy even for me. I completely misunderstood the gravitational pull of how my actions would have impacted my family, faith, and friendships.

Thank God for his grace and patience in a teenage rage.

# We the people have rights "without black codes"

The thirteenth amendment of the US constitution abolished slavery "within the United States, or any place subject to their jurisdiction." The senate passed it on April 8, 1864, the house on January 31, 1865, and it was ratified by the states on December 6, 1865. Congress required this for all former confederate states, including Georgia. (www. Constitution center.org)

Below are the thirteenth constitutional rights of all human beings residing in the United States of America.

❖ The right to be a human being without prejudice from bias minded people
❖ The right to be powerful in your own space
❖ The right to fight for what you believe in as long as it's a positive position of justice and truth
❖ The right to register to vote and vote without regrets
❖ The right to improve your life to impact your family, environment, and community
❖ The right to pursue your dreams without interference from negative bystanders
❖ The right to pursue your civil rights and take action to improve your quality of life without interference
❖ The right to fall in love without prejudice
❖ The right to worship in peace
❖ The right to protest in peace with bias
❖ The right to a free appropriate and proper education for all children
❖ The right to form alliances for good causes
❖ The right to live peacefully without negative distress from insecure people

# The entertainer's footprints

As fans of performers, we become enthralled with their abilities to ignite or quench the fires within our reservoirs.

They tickle our heart strings with clever lyrics and melodies, which touch our inner souls whether spiritual or secular.

They supply and entice us with music universally.

Although we are not privy to their living conditions, they intentionally live restrictively. What we see visually gives the appearance of glitter and gold. We fail to see any natural transparency.

It ain't always flashy and fancy, they too want to live respectably. The external glimpse and bits of glitter exhibited during their performances leaves us feeling as though we are complete with their reality. The behind-the-scenes injuries, and painful memories of insults and broken fantasies, stain their rightful human dignities.

In those moments when the demons come alive, they ride like a Clydesdale tracking the ghosts of yesteryears.

In a looking glass, they mirror a reflective message of liberation in spiritual personification.

Yes, musicians, singers, and entertainers give us reflections of who we want them to be.

Their music and movies cradle us in times of struggles and emotional rages.

Their music and movies strengthen us and lift us to magnificent heights in various stages.

In this place, we enjoy peace, tranquility, and the purpose of faith like supernatural grace.

# The reckoning with my reality (behind the orange curtain)

L iving in this world for over sixty years, I have done a bit of traveling throughout the country. I am an educated woman and an immigrant from Kingston, Jamaica. I have been in the United States of America for over fifty years and have experienced a predatory behavior from white society over time. I have dealt with misguided ideologies and uninformed interpretations from others with a lack of melanin in their skin tones. So, unfortunately, I'm not a stranger to tempered judgments. Some with malice, but mostly from fear or knowledge about whom they have not come in contact with. Usually, I'm able to shake off the uninvited notions of the predicting prejudice headed my way. But, today, I sincerely had to come to terms that when a person of a different culture and complexion walks into the crossroads of a culture clash, therein lies a potentially dangerous reckoning of sorts on my skin color.

Good lord, I'm black. It distinctly has a taste and a flavor of resentment. The possibility of a turning of the tides becomes real. I am in Newport Beach, California, waiting for my niece to recover from her surgery on this beautiful Friday morning. In my careful search for a place to sit and wait, my thoughts came to a gripping haunt.

With its calming, quaint, and charming personality, this beach community quickly reminded me of the staunch realization that I was a minority in this town, encompassed by people of lesser melanin. I immediately had to connect and reconcile that I may be at a disadvantage if someone decides that I am deemed unworthy to receive service in their place of business or establishment. This brutal truth brings a level of discomfort regarding prejudice, a reckoning that another human being should never have to confront on the face of this earth. I was profoundly disappointed in having to address a thought that had never crossed my mind in the past, ever! I had occasions when others imprisoned me mentally and tried to deny my place on the planet by serving another before me. And, yes,

I've had to become assertive in standing up for my right by reclaiming my dignity. But the natural realization of that possibility was fundamental for me today. I have always felt that no matter the environment. I could navigate through the situation. Today I had to rely on my faith in God's grace to redeem my confidence that no matter where I am, "I belong."

I am from an environment that strongly supports and promotes the advocacy of inclusion of everyone around us. However, today I thoroughly had to recognize and reconnect with the reality that other people with darker melanin encounter this tragedy, and experience this feeling of pre-traumatic stress disorder daily. Granted, I have not had the experience of being denied inclusion from the businesses in the area. Astonishingly, Black people have dealt with this debilitating disease for over two hundred years. I am floored by the absolute abomination of irrational thinking of those who live in the hollowness of a dark tunnel.

I did, however, meet one amiable gentleman from a culture close to mine. He was a security person from the Latino community. Our conversation put my mind at ease as I discovered that not all people carry the same disturbing sting toward people of darker melanin. It is a dreadful shame to think of the possibilities and potential interrelatedness missed, that have the potential to change the world significantly, on a global scale funneled with hypocrisy.

# The wind

Strong, marvelous and mighty with a tremendously powerful and unpredictable drive. It displays no precautionary features or measures of fearsomeness. It simply weaves a cantankerous gavel as it motions owning no weight, yet it is heavy in its movements. It stretches and bends objects like a woman in travail giving birth; expressing her pain and magnifying the point and pressure it brings in its ability to disturb, release, and redefine at the center of its core. Its presence is magnificent as it distributes and elicits incredible aromas leaving trails of intoxicating exotic smells of homemade meals. It stirs the soul tantalizing your nostrils with fragrances like roses, almond berries, and watermelon. It offers relief like no other can. This ladylike breeze you can feel in her present stance. You can hear it as it whistles to capture your attention. It pushes like a bull, but you cannot embrace it to retaliate. You can't touch it, but it touches you, and now I'm in a state of I can't relate.

It rushes through as it rumbles and stirs the bows of swaying palm trees, causing them to curtsy and dance like a scripted movie scene in the midst of a mad summer's fest. It moves with unconditional adherence as plants promenade gracefully and performs at its commands like a magistrate. The early morning joy of getting a glimpse of its possibilities igniting your imagination is unreal. It suspends your mind beckoning you to rest in its supernatural love. It's a glorious moment in a morning breeze, intertwined with its connection to the sun's glow. You revel as it conducts a magically orchestrated show, casting shadows of incredible delightful reflections in your window. It is a magical delight. The wind is strong in its perseverance, while it whispers in loud musical notes. It is alive, bringing turmoil or pleasure in any given situation or circumstance.

It lifts all living and nonliving particles within its reach. Given the opportunity, it demands and requires the attention of a two-ton truck, as it suspends it in mid-air. It is remarkable in its ability to move, shaping, and swirling sounds that invigorate your soul. Whether it's the Santa Monica or Santa Ana, it is a mind-blowing phenomenon. It zips across waters, causing them to rise and pivot without caution. It is majestic in its perfection to our sensations. It flows through windows and doors and creeps through openings, crevices, and, yet you cannot see, as it overflows. Can you hear it, as it whispers through your fingers? It is mighty having no remorse for fishermen, bringing them to a lull on the ocean's frontier. The wind sends a chill through your soul, turning and stopping you dead cold. It will overturn a cargo ship with one swift mighty unwelcomed kick.

The wind is God's gift to us, and as humans, we try to control its direction. It is gracious in its unchallenged mannerism, moving paper, leaves, rock, or a weathervane twelve feet deep in the ground. It moves organisms without prior notice, or a chance to swiftly hide. They are now twisted in a frown. The wind can turn pools into dust bowls without filtering the debris from its arms. It is a breath of fresh air on a hot summer's day, as it refreshes with its charm. It is freaky, crazy, wild, and beautiful when it finds you in an unexpected place. The wind is a mesmerizing wonder to behold on all facets. It is one of God's greatest astonishing captivating creations to cover earth's atmospheric rising. It is a scientific marvel, an electrifying incredible energy source yet to be untapped, if we are not too dividing. It is a gift of life. It is also surprising.

# White "people's" premise of privilege

In my dealings with the "white" identity and ideology, I have noticed that they have taken on the assignment of giving themselves the authority to assume the purpose and position of entitlement, according to the preverbal status of the hierarchical definition, "no one but me, do you understand?"

It must be a strain on your psyche to work so hard to take on the mentality of uprightness as a cause to insult others you think are reckless. You find it difficult to take responsibility for any behaviors committed by your white counterparts; so, you justify their behaviors to counterattack any fault of their actions is dysfunctionally your stand.

Have no fear. We're not perfect, but we are not impressed by your transactions of distress. As for you, white people, we are not impressed. People of all ethnicities do it, but people of lesser melanin have monopolized the cornerstone as a preying, paralyzing ambition. Your behavior is mirrored as an inherently disrespectful manner of garnering power to get attention. When and where were you given the right to thread on the head of your fellow human spirit?

It's funny that you don't see yourself as the enemy but envision everyone around you as you become their frenemies. By doing so, you set out to extort every possible means of life from other people you consider to be the dangerous ones to your lifestyle redundancies. I have a saying, and it goes like this, "how quickly the tables can turn."

During the Black Lives Matter movement, at the height of the 2020 pandemic, your hierarchical reign had the presence of weakening; therefore, it left you in a strain. At any rate, you immediately jumped into aggressive action to correct the reckoning. Your financial empowerment became threatened by the people you spent your lifetime subjecting to economic and social enslavement.

Their strength became their weapons of choice. They moved to retaliate, rejuvenated by their frustrations and disappointments, in the treatment you have vowed to deliver destructively, as they were the object of your ternary. It's ironic when the table is turned how you notoriously cry wolf based on feeling weary. When in fact, you're the wolves in sheep's clothing, just as in the fable of little red riding hood.

You perpetrate attacks and only we recognize that you're the attacker in every neighborhood. What will it take for you "white peoples" to realize and understand that this is not your land? You parade incognito, falsified information to confuse and conquer past and present occupants. Whether in position, wealth, or reputation, when will it ever end? Will we ever be friends?

We are not at your command. Do you understand? Because those that have suffered at your hands, have come to a place collectively, where your strength and power must no longer be an agonizing consumable grandstand.

# As we are

It garnered in me a significant amount of appreciation, gratitude, and a multitude of blessings to write this piece. I was inspired as I took in a remarkable journey through the eyes of an African princess, a woman of darker melanin. I witnessed her ambition without fear to educate her fellow sisters in the motherland, to embrace us as we are. Her inner and outer strength and growth were as transparent as glass. Her heroine act to help her sisters in transition was amazing as an actress in her craft, and her need to be reminded of her strong heritage was enough for me. I too was reminded as a young woman growing up in New Jersey, that we are not so distant in our struggles with self-images. It brought about my fears of not fitting in because of the color of my dark skin. I saw women regretful, mourning their reflection of mistakes as tears ran down their heavy hearts and cheeks.

From an outsider's perspective, their inner spirits were bleeding to be naturally recognized. Beverly Naya explored some reasons why the skin bleaching industry in Africa is a billion-dollar brutal financial empire. The documentary is simply called "Skin". (2019) Women immersed themselves in creams to lighten their skin, soaking in the white emulsion to change the complexion of a sun-kissed skin. I was taken aback to witness such a travesty in African women. It matters not the condition of your purse as one woman stated. The social impact of attaining complexion acceptance is number one on most Nigerian women's social calendars. The lighter you are the more relevant you seem to be. Assimilation to white imperialism is a common theme and issue for darker-toned women. How unreal is this pharmacy of hypocrisy white society has placed on the most beautiful women on God's earth? And the truth behind this emotional discrepancy is a financial empire that benefits the white financial bureaucracy. We must check our reality in John 7:24, "Do not judge by appearances, but judge with right judgment."

We must understand the bigger picture. We are being bamboozled completely because we are trained to think of ourselves as less than. Our attitudes as black, Nigerian or American women should not be of fear, but be that of the bear. It doesn't matter to me who you are, because I know who I am. Women of darker melanin, is it plausible to stop and think that we don't belong? Believe in the treasures that you are. You are a rare gem . You are God's designed, created, and fashioned in His image. You are remarkable and complete in the life you embody and love. You are the pillar others wish to be. You are strong, confident, respected, and God-fearing because you are the light that has come to be, a blessing in the shadows of a misguided, misinformed society. Whether you are born natives, grown locally, or imported internationally. Your destiny does not and should not exist or be defined because of the color of your skin. You are not a trophy, to be shelved like the remnants of a forgotten movie script. You are a beautiful human being, gifted with dimensions, suitable for queens and princesses. Your worth and measure come from your inner strength, not from the darkness, or lightness of your skin content. You are a gift plain and simple. You are creative, articulate, wise, engaging, witty, emotional, perplexing at times, but genuine in every aspect of your natural rhyme.

We are, as we are, empowered to be the embodiment of sensitivity. We are the assured resisters of your lack of transparency. We are the products of past and present histories. We are not unnatural defunct predicaments of your rejected territories. Our desire to give love and be reciprocated in love is the only prescription of relevancy needed in this malfunctioned society. Life is like a well-penned song; it never gets too old.

In the Song of Solomon 1:5 it says, "I am very dark, and lovely, O daughters of Jerusalem, like the tents of Kedar, like the curtains of Solomon." We are the daughters of King Solomon. Rise up, my sisters, and acknowledge your power and be courageous. We have progressed through adversities far beyond the colors of our epidermis. We are without a doubt far more valuable than any bottle of whitening cream will ever dismiss. Save your narratives, your dollars, and your Nairas to build your empires. Let the others scratch and scream, for they are nothing more than mere vampires. The richness of my skin tone is not seasonal. My darkness represents the hues of mahogany all around. Even though my epidermis, my color must never be repressed for my genealogy is magnificently contiguous for we are blessed.

# L A X, why am I in trauma?

Whether on arrival or departure, LAX has the inappropriate appearance of a disheveled old man. Has anyone ever noticed when entering the thoroughfare of Los Angeles international airport, it has the distinct smell of an old man in distress? You're left trying to identify what causes such a problem, such a mess. Its entrance is cumbersome and in constant need of upgrades and undergoing incomplete construction projects, which interferes with your passage to arrival or departure gates. The disastrous plan to give its customers a refreshing experience only puts you at a disadvantage.

In having a conversation with one of my nieces the other day, we concluded that LAX appears to be under a never-ending contract to keep the Angels in flight with thoughts of whether this will ever come to a closure or will we always be in strife. Will there be calm when entering its gates where passengers, whether arriving or departing, will experience a pain-free landing? No matter your mode of transport, be it public or private vehicles, we are hopeful. We are optimistic that the traffic will be smoother than the current system of stressful, dysfunctional, irritating situations. We are confident that the lack of parking and flights not directly connected to functional parking structures will eventually right itself. We hope that American Airlines and Spirit Airlines will hire folks sensitive to the needs of the people who furnish their salaries. We are confident that one day LAX will be a peaceful place to venture in and out without debris and regrettable entanglements, where one can enjoy a restful travel event. Why am I in trauma at LAX?

# Black love

I love black love when it's genuine, honest, and untampered. In our society, black love is rationalized as a unique dysfunctional system not to be experienced. You don't want to fall in love with a black man because he can't give love. There may be some in that category, but you can't allow white society to define your station in life. The world we live in was not built only on their standards, philosophy, or knowledge. Don't assume that it works only according to their intentions of intelligence. I am here to tell you that it's a mythical assumption. Every relationship has its ups and downs. But, if you, as a team, learn what you desire from each other, it only improves. Trust and respect are the cornerstones of your foundation of hope. Without those two columns, your house is weak and will eventually fall. When two people meet and find something that attracts one to the other, fear should not be a stumbling block that prevents progress. Because of your historical judgment attitude, sad mistakes, and misguided emotional setbacks, don't hold back. Make it each other's business to dismiss the myths and love irresistibly.

You don't shake it; you embrace it. It is undeniably motivating to see two people together romantically creating a full circle of life, generating so much richness. I am intrigued to see genuine integrity, unfiltered compassion, and selfless giving. Unbreakable is a statement of commitment. Relentless commitment, sensitivity, caring without hesitation. Loving unabashedly, and unwavering trustworthiness are strengths I admire. I am grateful and impressed.

I am not ashamed to be black when I encounter this treasured finding. It's a fantastic adventure worth fighting for, in my eyes. It's a fulfillment one dares to believe in, engage in, and invest in. Life is about giving thanks to each other for each other, holding on when others think you should let go. Keep the candles burning because your best is yet to be between you. Because when you know that you know, you know what you know is real.

Believe when others can't see what you believe in. Finding joy when things look like there should be no joy, allowing the music in your hearts to sink into each other's spirit. Celebrate with thanksgiving without cause because you know God's got your back.

That's what black love means to me.

# HUMANITY

## Assessing one's value

Think in terms of your perceived expectations. Ask yourself, to whom do you belong? Assessment is the process of incoming information, and outgoing responses be it in body language, verbal cues, or written expressions.

In every aspect of our lives, whether good or bad, you the individual are a willing participant (unless you have been subjected to extreme, and I mean, an extreme vulnerability in your circumstances). Aside from those instances, the responsibility solely lies in your hands and heart how you interpret the information you're receiving to influence the projected outcome. Because as information enters your ears, travels to your brain, it will impact your heart, your emotions, your thoughts, and your physical senses. It's up to you to identify and interpret and process what you have received in order to assess your next move.

Let me address this unpleasant domain in which you're now very present. It's a hard place to find yourself. You're ready to go into fight or flight status. Please give the incoming what feels like an attack, sincere and purposeful attention. It's absolutely revitalizing to stay in control. Though it may hurt like nothing else in the world, realize that you are valuable in every area of your life. Adjust your balance, bring your upright courage, and be present at the moment, especially if it's from a man who you have invested time and energy in. Your reaction will not be pleasant, with the realization that he's an impressionable imbecile. So, sit for a moment and let it sink into your most inner being. Gather your strength, then respond with a wellspring of intentional replies, replies that are steadfast in your core beliefs to maintain your sanity. And know that once you make the decisions you are about to verbalize, you are ready to move on with your dignity intact. God's got you in your moment of trial and truth right where you stand. It's important to believe that you are more than a conqueror, you are a child of the living God. So, let Him fight your battles against the enemy in every situation or angle that comes up against you, my sisters. You are more than enough when the foundation around you feels like you're now standing in a sinkhole. God's got you always! Jeremiah 29:11 says, "I know the plans I have for you declared the Lord, plans to prosper you and not to harm you, plans to give you hope and a future."

Live a life filled with God's grace and mercy, because humans are not without frustration and failure. Gratitude is your gift of greatness, and remember that your authority comes from God, not humans.

# Caught by a mouse

In this hour of my time as I live and dine caught in the net of a swift thinking pet.

I am slain in the trap of a mischievous mouse and its untimely petty set of underserving reckless tests.

In this house of repression, I'm going through a prayer of regression.

I'm caught in the net of a perplexed rat's spat. And I am unamused without a doubt.

I am just wondering why did I let him get out? He was far too intellectually challenging, reminding me of how much I shout.

I will never be caught by you, for you are an irrational control pent-up little spout. But here I lie looking as though I am unable to get free.

I will never surrender to this tiny creature's unbelievable tyrannical impractical shout; for he will be stung by a small unseen bumble bee hiding in the shame on my tree.

I am respectfully breaking free from this emotional rat trap.

I am a carnivorous mammal not a Swiss cheese-eating fragmented mental psychological unstrap bubble wrap. from in my kingdom,

I'm feared, yet I am captured by my own snare. I am a lion, hear me roar. I am powerful in my thoughts to open this illogically unsolicited fenced-in unpretentious mouse's door.

I really enjoyed writing this piece. It is the power of suggestion, not allowing small things to put you in a disadvantaged headspace of heartbreaks. You are more powerful psychologically than you sometimes tell yourself. Your inner strength is greater than anything that tries to leave you defenseless such as even a small mouse.

# Every life is a descendant from an earlier life

Here we are, my friends. I'm bringing you a brilliant quote from one of my favorite artists, Mr. Bob Marley. "The greatness of a man is not how much wealth he acquires, but in his integrity and ability to positively affect those around them." Freedom is a gift that can turn a crooked smile straight. It is entirely up to us to recognize and share our hearts with others. Some of us would instead set fire to the advantage of freedom rather than share it.

As said in the movie *Same Kind of Different as Me*. "We are all homeless migrants working our lives back home." But, too often, many of us are on a sullen journey. Life is the creation of our Heavenly Father, who established us unto His likeness. Homelessness may find us in a place of disbanded engagements or that of an abandoned spirit. But that life does not have to remain in a muddy stall. Mans' mind was intended to apply the concept of critical thinking, to capture knowledge to increase our learning opportunities. Unfortunately, sometimes life gets stolen by habits or by others with bad intentions. Unfortunately, some people with mangled intentions and biased intelligence destroy the seedlings before they can take root. They poison the very life that will one day save their own. Everyone has a story to tell, but unfortunately, some are prevented from expressing their experiences. Many are trampled upon simply by the color of their skins, while others hide the darkness of their hearts. A rootless nature is harder to reverse when the soul is missing, and the core is as cold as stone.

In the same way, it's God's will to tint the melanin of one's skin tone. I believe that God's lesson for all of us is that what's inside of us is more valuable than what's on the outside. Do we always know how someone becomes homeless, but should we even care about the circumstances that met them there? Maybe, but should it matter? Because the only thing that should matter is the love that exhibits and echoes a position of positive change in someone else's life.

# The deadliest kind of ambition

Ambition is that thing that moves you from a simple, sincere individual to a depraved beast. In life, ambition is beautiful to inspire and challenge your intentions, dreams, and desires, but only if conducted with integrity. You become impressed with tangible materials directly in your path. But are you aware of the deceit and deception that floats on the seas of destruction? You put your best effort forward, being committed to the upper classes. And, without question, your loyalty might just restrict your movements and hold you hostage. You become a pawn in the greater scheme of the upward climb to notoriety.

Your hard work and dedication are used against you as if you are dispensable, a useless throwaway. And by the time you realize what's going on around you, no doubt you're now prey looking to fight your way out of the tiger's mouth. Romans 1:28 identified the inevitable once we lose sight of God. "And just as they did not see fit to acknowledge God any longer, God gave them over to a depraved mind, to do those things which are not proper."

According to the Bible, humans are inherently different from animals. Animals aren't concerned about the bigger things in life like justice and mercy, fairness, and love. However, when life's experiences throw you in unexpected places, emotionally and physically, which negatively impacts your balance, it becomes a frightening contrast to the former you. At this juncture, resentment builds up and can harden the very soul you try to preserve. And unconsciously became a scar within your psyche. You engaged in sinister thinking, which becomes dangerous; you are now a vicious killer without a conscious effort.

How can a human being with earlier simple intentions be motivated by greed to intentionally reckless behavior? These manifested lousy character traits are the dark shadows we live with daily. We are responsible for our actions, good, bad, or ugly. What role does our conscious identity play in right and wrong decision-making processing? I watched a movie the other day and saw a man with a castle filled with hopes and dreams.

The unfortunate revelation of who he became to achieve those dreams challenged the more profound spirit that leads, drives or compels his train of ambition. He became numb to those around him, taking lessons from his immediate environment. He believed that his employers owed him; after all, he had sold his soul to protect their innocence and secrets. He was the killer no one saw coming. He climbed the ladder of success economically and socially with the blood of his employer's life on his hands.

Are we so sensual that we missed the clues? Is it possible to be so understated that everyone around him missed his cold-blooded intentions? Is it possible to carry out such a devious undertaking without one ounce of suspicion?

If you want to find the heart of a human, touch his soul by inhumanly macerating his/her spirit. There you will see who he is. Please let me know your thoughts on the subject. I know this sounds like a cliché, but the truth remains. "Hurt people, hurt people."

(Source: https://bible.knowing-jesus. (com/topics/The-Carnal-Mind)

# Sojourners in a passage called life

Humans are created by God, given an opportunity to seek and discover blessings of hope and a future. We travel through a birth canal into the hands of another human being, not left to our own devices for self-care and nurturing. We need sustainable attention to forge adaptable developments to thrive. We desire closeness and touch to form connections. Positive interactions with each other are the only solid tools for sustainable survival. Still, sometimes too many of us become enemies of our own hearts. The language and lessons given to us through spoken words in our ears travel to our hearts will either install the kinds of power to build positive positions of fortitude or create an empty space of hate. Hate is a heavy burden to carry for children, teenagers, young adults, or older individuals.

Hate challenges us to legitimately evolve if we choose to move forward. It is an unfortunate measuring stick used to divide and isolate us from one another. Hate is a device used as a tool derived from a place of inadequate desperation. This insurrection of incorrect cactus-type spikes is a displacement of thoughts that must be addressed in our society. Our place in society is orchestrated through trials originating from a temple that cradles our belief system. It is the cornerstone of who you become. Each household is represented, or misrepresented by attendants, whether you like them or not. They may include parent(s), older siblings, older adults, or people from various cultures, which stabilize you whether you leave an honorable mark of positive possibilities or one of perilous despair. As humans, we were designed to create bonds, build bridges, and solve problems with thanksgiving, not become self-identifiers of grievances. Some souls are benched on a false ideology and have the audacity to reject someone as different, either in looks, skin tones, physical make-up, or intellectual capacity and capabilities. Our strengths are in the relationships we forge, not from the negative divisions we form. We are sojourners in a wilderness of a beautiful landscape on a planet called earth.

In Luke 17:20, when the Pharisees asked Jesus when will the kingdom of God come? He answered and said, "the kingdom of God is within you." This is God's providence waiting to manifest in our hearts.

My question is why and when did it occur to another human being that currency was the sum account of ownership of another humankind? Can you breathe into another human soul to revive a dead man or woman? No, I don't believe I have witnessed those miracles as yet. Has anyone? If so, give your account and demonstration of such events. The Bible shattered that assumption when it detailed how we were created. God blew His breath into a clay vessel and named it man. Human to be exact. That creation was not submitted through the hands of humans! So, I am astonished as to the audacity and tenaciousness of man to become so toxic in believing that any human soul can be bought and sold as cattle on a farm to be used as domesticated animals.

We were created for greatness even as we go about doing the small and mundane things in life, even when times seem futile in the process. As humans crawling was our first basic inherent behavior, we didn't learn to crawl by our parents getting down on their hands and knees and teaching us to crawl. God gave us that gift before we were born. In the stages of our development, we collectively exhibited the skill of walking as evident in this journey of life's gifts. Our learning modalities instilled and instituted should be from the hearts and shoulders of those who inspired us to be a blessing, not a curse. Those who did not see that in the lives they touched cheated any child of a tremendous transition of undelivered dreams. They were unfaithfully determined not to see the best in that person. Our journeys take many forms, from the risk of forming our first words to delivering a complete sentence; to the challenge of scientific accomplishments in all areas of our learning. Yet too many of us spend useless time on pointless thinking. Why? There are so many other opportunities to encounter, overcome and accomplish.

Instead, you put yourselves in a position of hopeless division rather than finding a good purpose to fight for. We can never imagine how God will intervene and connect us with a person or people to formulate a journey unimaginable to others. It should never be our intention to be exclusive or exclude opportunities or possibilities to teach, touch, and inspire life. There are three kinds of people: the kind who will risk from the heart with courageous engagement love and gratitude; the second will prey on others because of their own insecurities, they become abusers and life takers; and the third will fall to the grave denying themselves the opportunity to experience an unexpected journey of learning through the joys and trials they could have encountered.

Here is one example of a person with courage. A man in New York in 2000 minding his own business came upon an unexpected opportunity to fortify a young child's life. He made the decision to help redeem life to greatness. He made a choice and changed the life of a baby left in a subway by a coward unwilling to take a risk.

Another person chose to pass on that same opportunity because they were unwilling or lacked the courage to take that risk. This journey is unpredictable for all of us. Risking the willingness to embrace a task is assumed as a daunting undertaking because too many of us including myself at times resist the code of honor. So, count joy in every sorrow because that's right where He will be. Fear is said to be the table of division. If allowed, it will swallow up every morsel of your mortal fiber. Please, for the sake of our future, and the future of the planet we refer to as home, stop giving a place and purpose to things that are irrelevant to our time and our sojourn on earth's surface. We do not remain on its topsoil forever. We are renters of a place we did not create. So please remember to treat each life with thanksgiving, care, love, compassion, and grace. As we are only sojourners in a passage called life; don't forget to live it with conviction, consistency, confidence, courage, commitment, and consideration for the lives God put in front of you anytime in any space.

# I'm intrigued

It's impossible not to embrace the varying dynamics of my fellow humankind. I'm a people watcher. I'd be curious to know your status. I'm not sure if you might consider yourself an avid observer or not. But I enjoy watching how the mind and body work in tandem. The human species is a complicated mix of physical, emotional, and machinery. In my observation, humans tend to intermingle with intricate reluctance and patterns of unintentional compliance. And are interesting as a species sometimes deeply removed from each other's cultures. Although I am baffled about the process of how we engage with others outside our perimeters, I am left wondering sometimes. When I'm in my not-so-obvious state of observation of others around me, I notice little quirks of their obsessions. We move like water flowing and reseeding in and out of the ocean or the bay. We ebb and flow in various streams and stages, crossing rocks and pebbles sometimes without touching. It's incredible how folks generously open themselves to their riveting, emotional traumas, and unresolved vulnerabilities unknowingly.

The human experiences come into play in places and spaces we occupy, such as the grocery stores, a line in the bank, a classroom, the park, the car dealership, or the car wash. I reflect on the clothes they wear to their unconscious body language delivered, even during a short conversation, in restaurants, at outdoor events, at the dinner table, at the bar, or even at the gas station. Their curiosity or their shallowness shows up unexpectedly. I'm so intrigued by the smallest visibility in those open windows; it's inspiring. Some look for places to hide, some seek to make friends, some seek to overpower others, and others seek to find empowerment. Some seek validation, and some simply seek attention to justify their thirst and reasoning. And, if you're like me, you just want to take care of business and move on. Am I lying, people?

It is intriguing to me; I'm impressed by these bits of invulnerable, involuntary slices of the human spirit on canvas. As I watch the pictures move in various directions, I appreciate our vitality. I'm vividly clear, however, too many people seek to get noticed in the most surprising places. We might display our attitudes in a stance, a look, a gaze, a stare, a touch, a shuffle, or the way we sit. Or I'll take my damn time if you don't mind. Humans give so much of themselves away unknowingly or unintentionally.

Why are we interested, pretentious, scary, filled with ambivalence, loving, courageous, caring, combative, and fierce? Yet, we lack empathy for someone else's pain and suffering. I'm simply fascinated with the human psyche. Some people just pursue a more evident mindset and confidence, while others search to challenge others without a doubt to stronghold them. We all play a poignant role in this landscape of life on earth ! However, I'm just one that finds our interactions with one another's persona significantly intriguing. Are you a personal people watcher too?

# It looks like competition, but the reflection is fear

Whether it's in your place of employment, driving down the street, or in the grocery store, it looks like innocent competition. Walking up to the checkout, walking to get in line at the bank, or waiting in line on the playground, it looks like innocent competition. If a woman sees a man with another woman walking, her secret impulse kicks in to one up that woman. The same applies to men; they instantly see a woman with a great-looking man, and the drive to conquer sets in. The unthinkable reveals itself when you're heading to the bar in a pub, in line at the post office, or even during a conversation. Someone must exercise their assumed personal edge to be ahead.

I often wondered why. What causes someone to have such hunger for misplaced confidence to be a captive audience of self-righteousness? What is the motivation for this human behavior? I must be first in my head, it's them or me, and I will not allow someone else to win. This insatiable push to insert competition is accurate, no matter the place or circumstances we find ourselves.

That assertion must have an origin, so I had to take a step back and observe some of my colleagues, classmates, family members, and even friends. I then realized that we carry a void that demands reassurance of needed security in the form of aggression under the pretense of assertiveness. If I don't feel like I'm winning, I am not good enough. This fear of being left behind appears to be a temporary need to satisfy a profoundly emotional, central critical place of less than belonging. Fear is a dangerous path to find yourself locked in. As humans, we desire a clear zone of prominence, so we assume the position of me before you. When in fact, it is an overindulgence, a byproduct of inflated false personification. That misguided machine becomes the motivator, which then pushes our buttons and pressures us to feel superior.

We must quench our starving appetite of unfulfilled desired admiration. As humans, we crave adoration at all times. What is the need once we feel disrespected? We create a space of selfish assertion to one-up someone else in that desperate moment. The Bible is an anchor we need to survive on the planet in harmony.

Philippians 2:3-4 directs us to the following: "Do nothing from rivalry or conceit but count others more significant than yourselves in humility. Let each of you look not only to his interests but also to the interests of others." Ezekiel 34:18 states, "Is it not enough for you to feed on the good pasture, tread down with your feet the rest of your pasture; and drink of clear water that you must muddy the rest of the water with your feet?" Why do humans behave like animals snared in a net, as though captured as wounded prey? Is it an innate intellectual dysfunction that seeks cognitive alignment, or just some superficial ego trip seeking superimposed greed to control our space, the moment, or event? Is it an impractical functionality of our marginal imagination?

I wondered why people continue to display a desperate need to exercise competition, or is it simply an unresolved measure of insecurity we possess? Do we innately carry hidden guilt to be recognized boundlessly? I pray that I will admonish my actions of self-importance, surrender them, and consider others before me when tempted to secretly compete with them, even when done without their knowledge. I will let go and let God direct my blueprint in the future. Will you?

# The weed that serenaded the rose

Weeds spring up between the cracks and the crevices of an assumed flower bed. Flowers are precious, warm, and tender expressing the delicacy of life. Weeds, however, are pretentious, and woolly. They bring a certain kind of ruggedness to the garden's variation. The appealing richness and beautiful mix of the soothing colors and aromas airlifted from the rose; serenaded the nostrils of the exciting weed.

One can see the weed as it swirls and stretches its pretentious arms around the natural rose, caressing and tingling the life out of her. At this point, the poor rose is in a state of calmness and serenity. Weeds pop up pretending to be flowers, inserting anxiety because they are not there to provide support; they are there to stifle the growth of the flowers they encounter. They pretend to be cooperative, lending intimacy as if they are a part of the landscape. They invade, they intermingle, while they're competing to see who will thrive.

Relationships are much like a rose garden. Some men enter your life seeking out your vulnerabilities, rendering trauma like an obsessive weed. They surround you with a vagueness, a smile, a line from a well-researched song. They form an intimacy with your spirit just like a weed in the garden pretending to care, with a plan to choke, derail, and kill your inspiration and affection. It's unjust how a weed can pop up and survive among life in the garden of creation, disrupting the living. Relationships can be like a complicated mix of selfish ambitions, ambiguities, and uncertainties. Sometimes life upsides and provokes us as we become incredibly unaware of the disadvantages laid out before us. It's like the untold addiction we affiliate with.

We find ourselves in denial with the idea that we are underqualified to reside in its presence. I can't help that some men fear genuine relationships; they come off as charming. Still, they are perpetrators trading affections, seeking companionship without authentic realization of a lasting, uncomplicated functional relationship. Please encounter your fears before engaging in any meaningful long-term emotional intimacy. If you wish to indulge in chaotic endeavors, be honest and truthful to your integrity before setting your sights on another person's values and morals.

# Discovering values

So often, we go through life never respectfully addressing its rightful place. The clandestine lack of value we misplace on life gets wasted as we are perpetually perplexed while perpetrating fraud with disgrace. Time travels without a passport. It takes off and lands where we don't understand. It's unfortunate how some remain detached, waiting to hear when to land in their circumstance. In contrast, others hold material belonging as appendages, fastened with master locks keyed with an edge-less bandage.

We carry attitudes of self-serving ambitions, with no confidence in how to achieve within perplexing conditions. Life assignments include assuredness of prosperous, powerful endeavors and meaningful lessons of life's love letters. Life is remarkably more than just material blessings.

We get better when values are revealed as intrinsic rewards through relationship bonding. Hard work comes when one is willing to let go of selfish relations and have an open heart to the many values life holds throughout its remarkable renditions.

# Water is a living source

Water is transparent, inorganic, unappetizing, scentless, and uninteresting to sight. Yet, it is a living body with two distinct elements.

The following is a description of "Water" : it is an inorganic, transparent, tasteless, odorless, and nearly colorless organism. It doesn't sound like much, does it? But wait a minute! May I venture to ask? When do we consider water in its pure and natural form? What generally comes to mind? For me, it's a force to be reckoned with, and it compels me to think beyond any failure that may suppress my heart or mind. It is a regeneration of my optimism.

Water poses a strength that challenges our very way of life, and without it, we cannot survive. Even in its vaporized state, it is powerful enough to keep us on guard. When I think of water, it brings a level of security and fear alike; without a shadow of a doubt, it is one of the most intriguing elements on planet earth .

Water washes, quenches our thirst, and is a cleaner to things such as gold and silver. It bends iron and melts sand into glass. It is found in the likeness of rain, which appears to pour down from an opening in the sky above. It brings with it melodic sounds in low and subtle lyrics. Its looks can be subtle, deceiving, and appealing, all simultaneously. And, all the while, in the swiftness of a moment, it can move in strong currents carrying an unsuspecting dark side. Water refreshes. It sustains our daily lives. It can be deceiving to have the appearance of being docile in the form of a stream, a drip, a shower, or a small flow. The magnificent power it contains can drown you in as much as a tablespoon. And, yes, as humans, we take it for granted; we lack gratitude for its benefit toward our survival.

We visit the ocean because of its healing properties and possibilities. The joy of just touching your feet in it gives you such a rush, a peace not obtained in any other sense. It transforms your thoughts and transpires a blessing that ignites an exquisite pleasure no matter your state of mind. In my prayers, water represents a connection to God's goodness, grace, and mercy. It offers a place of safety, a sanctuary, an assurance of tranquility no other element presents. Just as our Father in heaven brings an electric charge to our souls, water washes away the old and offers us an opportunity for renewable energy. Water combines **hydrogen and oxygen**, and it exists in gaseous, liquid, and solid states.

Water is one of the most plentiful and essential compounds, occurring as a liquid on Earth's surface under normal conditions. It makes it invaluable for humans, plants and animals. To be able to jump in its melodic range and dance to a musical beat, which harbors a density of distinctive dynamic perspective should be a time to rejoice in the hope for a different outcome. Instead, we neglect its purpose and tend to take it for granted. In the essence of who God is telling us in the scriptures, He is the living water of our very existence. John 4:14 says, "But whoever drinks of the water that I will give him shall never thirst, but the water that I will give him will become in him a well of water springing up to eternal life."

As scientists would say, water is "bonded." Atoms bond together, forming molecules. (conversation.com) So, are we bonded together in spirit with Christ if we choose to believe and become one with Him? The following quote says it all for me. What are your thoughts? "Nothing is softer or more flexible than water, yet nothing can resist it." (Author unknown) The ironic thing about water is that we can drink as much of it as we like, and never gain weight. Just as Christ offers a place in Him never bloats our egos or swells our need for mindless influences. He provides us with a destiny of greatness and a richness humans will never understand. A remarkable substance we as humans cannot bring to the table under any circumstances. So, in my feeble attempt to reach a deeper understanding of the power water holds, I look to my Father's strength, His spirit, where we can all claim His power because His water is a living source.

Reference:
https://www.britannica.com
the conversation.com
https://bible.knowing-jesus.com

# About the Author

I am Merice, the daughter of migrant parents from Jamaica, W.I. My parents were explorers. They traveled the seas to discover their love, passions, and gifts. My grandparents were monumental in setting the precedence for overcoming obstacles through perseverance and God's provisions. They were about having faith, giving love, finding value in life, education, and trust in family. My parents passed these principles on to their seven children. Most importantly they taught us that service to others will be more beneficial than to oneself.

I am a versatile student advocate with over 30 years of professional educational experience, working in a student-focused learning environment. I am a determined advocate with aspirations to motivate everyone around me, as an enthusiastic life changer. My purpose in life, if you will, is to help, whether in the classroom, or in my community. My aim is to empower people to focus and achieve their greatest potential. I strive to provide assistance to special-education students with guidance as they succeed in the areas of literacy, adaptability, resourcefulness, and creativity.

Raising my daughter as a single parent was one of the greatest, life-changing gifts God gave me. Alex is now a practicing psychologist in Los Angeles. I have served as an anchor, instructor, and advocate to college students for the past five years. I am an insurance agent with the State of California, an employment specialist that prepares students for competitive markets in mainstream society as well as globally.

One might say I am a mentor who chooses to engage teens, young adults, and people overall. My greatest joy is to incorporate critical thinking skills to help others maximize their abilities for greater opportunities. I am a life-changing advocate in the Los Angeles South Central area to students in the Mama Hill's Help after-school program. It is my goal to be inclusive of all lives because all lives matter! I am proudly adding "Author" to my resume!

"My hope is my work will cause you to think, take action, and find a space to be an influencer with solutions."

Made in the USA
Las Vegas, NV
01 November 2022

58569792R00068